Steve,
Life's an
adventure
you for joining me on this
journey!

The BLACKOUT

A Novel Inspired by True Events

LOUISE ARSENEAULT

This book is inspired by true events. However, to protect the privacy of certain individuals, names and identifying details have been changed. Please note that some characters are the composition of the author's imagination and have been created to develop the story.

The book reflects the author's recollections of experiences over time and her interpretation of conversations that took place. The opinions expressed within this book are the author's personal opinions and are merely "freedom of expression."

Cover design by Romana Bovan

Tellwell Talent
www.tellwell.ca

ISBN
978-0-22881-478-8 (Hardcover)
978-0-22881-477-1 (Paperback)
978-0-22881-479-5 (eBook)

TABLE OF CONTENTS

DEDICATION

This book is dedicated to Jeannine, Lynn, and Daniel, whose kindness and generosity I could never repay.

To my mom, Suzie, and my dad, Michel, for your unyielding love and support.

To my brother, Patrick, for being my best friend and an example of loyalty.

And to you, my wonderful reader, for joining me on this adventure of growth.

ACKNOWLEDGEMENTS

Writing this book has been an incredible journey of growth and self-discovery. Such a project, with all its details and intricacies, would not have been possible without help and support.

It is with a warm heart and sincere appreciation that I give special thanks to those mentioned below who have made this process successful and assisted me in reaching my goal.

To my mom, Suzie Arseneault, for your endless support and encouragement. The hours we spent reading and revising brought me great laughter and joy. I am grateful for all that you have done and I thank you for helping me make this dream a reality.

To Jeannine Caissie and her wonderful children, Daniel and Lynn, for your everlasting impact, love and kindness.

To my good friend, Casey Mims, for your honest opinions and numerous "*Cake*" readings.

To my amazing editing team: Shelley Mascia, Caitriona McBride, Roxana Coumans, Jenny Hong, and Mary Washington. I can't thank you enough for your patience and skills.

To my cover designer, Romy, I am forever grateful for your creativity and attention to detail.

Finally, to all my friends, family, and host families, thank you for sharing this journey with me and being a source of constant support and encouragement. Your loyalty and kindness run close to my heart, and it is an honor to have you all be a part of my life.

CHAPTER 1

THE TAKEOFF

"Yes Mom, I promise I'll be safe."

"Okay honey, but make sure you call me as soon as you land and be careful!"

"Mom, how many times are you going to say that?"

"As many times as I need to comfort myself." I sighed, hugging my mother one more time. "I love you sweetheart."

"I love you too, Mom. Now let me go before I miss my flight!"

She smiled gently, wiping a tear from her cheek. I turned and placed my backpack on the conveyor belt. I couldn't believe this was actually happening.

"Please step forward, miss." The agent motioned for me to step through the metal detector.

My heart began pounding as I anxiously obliged. I paused past the hollow frame as the agent's hand motioned for me to stop. I stared at him wide-eyed, wondering what I had done wrong, but he wasn't looking at me. I followed his gaze and glanced over my shoulder. The metal detector light was red, but suddenly it turned green. I let out a sigh of relief.

"Have a good flight," he stated, his voice monotonous. Fearing that he would change his mind, I quickly grabbed my backpack and disappeared into the crowd.

Once safely out of sight, I pulled out my boarding pass. *Gate B10.* I glanced up at the suspended signs, and to my delight, I was right where I needed to be.

Proud of myself for not looking like an inexperienced traveler, I took the first open seat in front of my gate. I placed my backpack on my lap and attempted to make myself as small as I could. The lady to my left smiled gently, and I shyly smiled back. To my right was a well-dressed gentleman in a three-piece suit, staring down at his laptop. I wondered why he was so well dressed. Seated in front of me were a row of teenagers who seemed to be anxiously waiting for time to pass, and I wondered if all of them had flown before.

I looked over my shoulder for the gate agent, but she was nowhere to be found. I glanced at my watch; I still had thirty minutes before the first boarding announcement. *I still have plenty of time.*

One of the ladies in the row in front of me sneezed, and I immediately looked up. I was about to say "bless you," when waving hands from behind the glass wall, caught my attention. I ducked forward as the glare of the sun made it hard for me to make out who it was. To my disbelief, it was my mother.

Horrified, I shrank down in my seat while she smiled victoriously. I wondered how long she had been standing there making herself look like a fool. I guess it didn't matter. She had succeeded at getting my attention, and now

I couldn't take my eyes off of her. She pointed to her eye, pointed to her heart, and then pointed at me. I put both of my hands out to my side and shrugged my shoulders.

"What?" I mouthed.

The lady who had sneezed earlier stared at me, looked over her shoulder, and then stared at me again in confusion. I was utterly embarrassed.

Tap, tap, tap. Somehow I managed to hear my mom knocking on the glass.

"What?!" I mouthed again, irritated.

She repeated her earlier sequence with a radiant smile on her face, as if I had agreed to a game of charades. I forced a smile trying my best to chase away the desire to disappear and urged my brain to decode her self-made sign language.

Suddenly, I understood her message. She pointed to her eye: *I.* She pointed to her heart: *love.* She pointed to me: *you.*

Slightly ashamed that I had allowed her to work my nerves, I replied. I pointed to my eye: *I.* I pointed to my heart: *love.* I pointed to her: *you*, and I held up the peace sign for her to see: *too.*

My mom smiled tenderly, holding both hands together as if she was sending me off to college. Although I couldn't quite grasp what she saw when she looked at me, I knew she was thinking, "My baby is growing up."

She was right. I was growing up. I had just turned fourteen years old and this was my first time flying. My mom's sister, Aunt Sherry, lived on the other side of the country, and she had asked me to spend the summer with her, her husband, and her two toddlers. Having the innate desire to travel the world, I had excitedly agreed.

By the skin of my teeth, I had made the mandatory age cutoff and chosen not to travel with an accompanied flight attendant. My mom had been reluctant to have me travel alone, but with a bit of persuading, I had succeeded in convincing her that I was mature enough and ready to conquer the nine-hour trip with one layover.

"Ladies and gentlemen, this is a boarding announcement for Flight 456 with service to Hamilton. At this time, we would like to welcome all passengers seated in Zone 1. Again, all passengers seated in Zone 1, please make your way to gate B10. Thank you."

The gate agent was now standing behind her desk. To ease my mind, I looked at the flight number listed on the screen above her and confirmed it with my ticket. *This is it,* I thought, excitement fluttering in my stomach. I searched my boarding pass for my assigned zone number. I was seated in Zone 2. I took a deep breath in anticipation.

"Ladies and gentlemen, we are now welcoming passengers seated in Zone 2. Passengers in Zone 2, please make your way to gate B10. Thank you."

A thrill ran through me. This was it! It was my first time standing at an airport gate. It was my first time standing in this sort of line, and it was my first time boarding a plane. With the excitement of adventure running through my veins, I got up and stood in line.

After patiently inching my way to the desk, I handed my ticket to the gate agent who smiled and swiped it. *Beep.* I watched as the red light from the scanner turned green. I was once again cleared to proceed. I placed my hands on my backpack straps and took a deep breath—I was ready.

I had just taken a step towards the tunnel when the thought of my mom crossed my mind. At the gate agent's announcement, I had forgotten all about her. I looked over my shoulder and the man in the suit huffed, impatient for me to proceed. I couldn't. I stepped aside allowing him to pass me. He scoffed.

The tiny voice in my head spoke out my worst fears. I couldn't ignore them. *What if this is the last time you'll see her? What if the plane crashes? Any last words?*

I searched through the window for my mom, who was lovingly waiting for one last glance. Inexplicably, all my fears vanished. I knew that I would be okay. I watched as her face lit up with pride. I waved and smiled at her brightly. I blew her a kiss, turned around, and headed down the airport tunnel.

The flight attendant smiled at me from inside the plane, and I couldn't help but admire her attire. She wore a navy skirt with a white button up, along with a yellow scarf tied around her neck. *Just like the movies*, I thought, stepping into the aisle.

I walked the narrow passage all the way down to my seat, *17*A. There, a middle-aged lady with curly gray hair was attempting to stuff her luggage in the overhead compartment above my seat. The way she was hitting and shoving her bag made me assume that she was either nervous or flustered. With it bursting at the seams, it was no wonder that she was struggling. Finally, she gave it one last hard shove and by some miracle managed to fit her entire bag into the designated compartment.

"I'm sorry," she mumbled, taking her seat.

Before I could stop her, her trembling hands had grabbed a hold of the seatbelt and she was buckled in. A line was now forming behind me, and I began sharing her nervousness.

"Umm, excuse me. I'm in that seat," I said, nodding to the open space beside her.

As frantically as she had sat down, she unbuckled herself and sprang up. With little space to maneuver and with the line of impatient people growing behind us, we managed to perform some sort of forced waltz by facing each other and turning simultaneously, allowing me to take my assigned seat.

I took off my backpack and stuffed it underneath the seat in front of me. I had just buckled myself in, when I caught sight of the curly-haired lady sitting erect. She was buckled in with both hands gripping the armrest for dear life. *We're not even airborne yet,* I thought, partially wondering what the rest of this flight would be like.

Ding.

"Ladies and gentlemen, my name is Captain Cooper. Welcome aboard Flight 456 with service to Hamilton, Ontario. Current temperature in Hamilton is 18 degrees Celsius. Flight time today is three hours and fifty-four minutes. We advise you to remain seated with your seatbelt safely fastened while the seatbelt light is on. Unfortunately, we are foreseeing a bit of turbulence about midway through this flight, but we will do our best to ensure that everything else in our control goes smoothly. We will be airborne shortly. Thank you."

From the corner of my eye, I watched as the curly haired lady's chest rose up and stopped. She was holding her breath. I could tell she was terrified and immediately I felt like a veteran flyer.

"First time flying?" I asked, smiling politely. She nodded, staring straight ahead. "Mine too," I added.

Her eyebrows rose in surprise as she slowly turned towards me. She looked at me up and down before taking a deep breath.

"I'm Lucy," I stated, holding out my hand.

"Deborah," she replied, reluctantly putting her hand into mine. I shook it firmly.

"Nice to meet you," I smiled.

The plane started moving and Deborah tensed up again.

"So, where are you heading?" I asked. I knew that forcing her into a conversation would help her make it through takeoff.

"Ehh, Hamilton," she answered.

"Cool, I have a layover there. I'm headed to Kelowna." She stayed silent. "So, do you have family in Hamilton or something?"

She smiled faintly, and I noticed that the tip of her fingers were no longer white. She was finally beginning to relax.

"I do, actually. My son moved out there with his wife a few years ago. I promised him that I would visit, but my fear of flying had me finding all sorts of excuses."

"Oh . . . " I nodded. "So what made you change your mind?"

Her face lit up with pride. "My son's wife just gave birth to a baby boy. His name is Walker. He is my first grandchild, and I told myself that I would overcome my fear . . . even if it kills me."

"Wow! Walker is a very lucky baby," I grinned.

The plane took up speed and the next thing I knew I was leaning backwards at a 45-degree angle, pressed down in my seat. We were airborne. My heart pounded as the distance between the plane and the ground grew at a steady pace. This was so amazing.

I stared out the window and for the first time in my life, I could see the world firsthand from a bird's-eye view. The blue sky, the fluffy clouds, the horizon, I had never seen anything like it. It took my breath away.

Suddenly, I felt a hand on mine, making my body jolt in surprise. Deborah was having a completely different experience. The look in her eyes was one of grave fear.

"It's okay Deborah. You're doing great." I squeezed her hand. She nodded and forced a smile.

My ears popped from the pressure, and suddenly, the sound of the plane's engines became faint. I could hear my breathing louder than ever before. It was as if I had just entered a soundproof room confining me solely to the sound of my being. It was strange, but I didn't mind it.

The plane leveled again as we reached cruising altitude. Deborah released my hand, and I was drawn towards the window again. The world below me was so small, and for a moment, I was lost in its beauty.

Ding.

The seatbelt light turned off, bringing me back to reality. Still deafened by the pressure change, I watched as a few people got up from their seats in the direction of the lavatory.

For the first time in my life, I could hear the tiny voice in my head loud and clear. *You know you're lucky? You just turned fourteen and you have the privilege to travel already. Many people will never have this kind of opportunity.*

I looked at Deborah, whose eyes were shut, and wondered what she was thinking. Was she sleeping? Was she praying? Was she regretting her decision? What was on her mind? Walker?

The flight attendant appeared in the aisle, pushing a cart. She stopped in front of my row and spoke. I stared at her and smiled, unable to make out her words. It was as if she was speaking underwater. I swallowed hard and wiggled my ear in an attempt to regain my hearing, but nothing. She tried again, this time holding up two bags—one filled with peanuts, the other with pretzels.

"Pretzels, please."

The sound of my voice was muffled but the attendant heard me perfectly. She reached across Deborah, handed me my snack and addressed me again. I assumed it was for something to drink.

"Apple juice, please."

The attendant smiled and handed me my drink before skipping over Deborah and addressing the next passenger. I sighed and glanced at my seatmate whose eyes were still shut. *I guess she's sleeping*, I thought, splitting open my pretzel bag. I paused for a second, "These must be the tiniest things I've ever seen," I whispered, pouring a few in my hand. *Better than nothing I guess*, I thought, tossing them in my mouth.

I had just washed the pretzels down with a gulp of my juice, when my left ear popped loudly. I winced in pain and tugged at my ear. My earlier deafness had vanished, and it was now replaced by the humming sound of the plane's engines. I could hear the chatter of the couple in front of me, and I wished I could return to the stillness of my thoughts.

As suddenly as my ear had popped, the plane dipped down without the slightest warning. In a jolt, Deborah gasped for air and the pit of my stomach felt as if it was on fire. *What had just happened?* Before I could think any further, the plane dropped again, spilling the apple juice all over my tray table.

Ding. The seatbelt light came on.

"Ladies and gentlemen, we are entering a rough area and we ask that you remain seated with your seatbelt fastened. Thank you for your cooperation."

The plane jerked forward, and half of the passengers screamed. I panicked. Strapped in my seat, bound to the plane, I was helpless. I had never felt anything like this before. The plane dropped again, and I felt like I was a on a roller coaster plummeting towards the ground. My mind raced as I thought about my dad, my mom, my brother, and my sister. I looked out the window at the thick black clouds that had replaced the shining sun, as if the earth was mourning an unexpected loss. *Was this for me?*

The plane rattled as it fought against nature to keep us steady. In an instant, my short life flashed before my eyes, but I refused to believe this was the end. Mentally, I fought back. *This is all part of the experience. You are going to be fine. This is just a test. Be brave. You have so much more of the world to see.*

I repeated those words until I calmed down. In some way, I knew I would be okay. Ignoring my own fears, I reached out and grabbed Deborah's hand.

"We're going to be okay, you know," I stated softly. I needed her to believe along with me. "Someone's watching over us. We're going to make it, I just know it!" She nodded while tears streamed down her cheek, but I could tell she was still paralyzed by fear. Wanting her to focus on something else, I continued, "Think about Walker and what he'll be like. Just keep your mind on him, you're going to be fine."

The plane dropped again, and Deborah opened her eyes. She took a deep breath and stated, "Yes, you're right. We're going to be fine." Her soft voice reminded me of my great-grandmother, and I couldn't help but smile.

"Now, let's just ride this thing out!" I exclaimed. Deborah took another deep breath and smiled sincerely.

As suddenly as the turbulence had quaked us, it was gone. I glanced out the window and the dark cloud that earlier engulfed us had dissipated. The dense fog became lighter as the sun peeked through, kissing my window once more. It was then that it dawned on me, *It had been there the entire time, as an ever-present light in the midst of a storm.*

I nodded, knowing that life had just taught me a valuable lesson. I was proud of myself for facing the demon named Fear. I knew from experience that he was a liar, but he hadn't paralyzed me. Instead, his voice had been but a momentary whisper that I had chosen to silence.

CHAPTER 2

CAREFUL WHAT YOU WISH FOR

The days in Kelowna flew by faster than I was able to spell summer vacation. From swimming in lakes to horseback riding, I had done it all. Now my amazing summer was coming to an end, and I couldn't believe that this was my last dinner with my relatives.

"So, did you have fun?" my aunt asked, serving me a heaping spoonful of spaghetti.

"Are you kidding me? I had a blast!" I said, swirling the noodles around my fork.

"Good," she smiled, serving herself. "It was a pleasure having you here, and we're sure going to miss you."

My little cousin screamed from his high chair as he had just dropped his sippy cup. "Here you go little guy," I said, handing him his juice. Sean smiled and uttered some incoherent babble. "No way, tell me more."

"See, that's exactly what I mean, we are going to miss you," she said.

I smiled and blushed a little knowing that I, too, was going to miss them. I returned to my seat and took a massive bite of spaghetti.

"So, Lucy, what are you doing next summer?" my uncle asked, making my aunt and I giggle.

"Oh, I don't know yet . . . " I mumbled, my mouth half full. "If I'm lucky, maybe I'll get to travel across the country again to spend time with my favorite relatives." I winked and took another bite.

"Tom!" my aunt yelled.

My uncle had slurped up one of his noodles, splattering sauce all over his chin. I did my best to muffle my laughter, but it was too late. I took a deep breath, but nearly choked on the food that was in my mouth.

"Lucy, are you okay?" my aunt asked, tapping me on the back.

"I'm fine," I coughed, taking a sip of my water.

At this point, my uncle was laughing so hard that it was nearly impossible not to join him. There was no denying it: I had spent an amazing summer with awesome people.

My alarm rang early that next morning, and I instantly regretted going to bed late. Groggily, I got up and shuffled to the bathroom. Eyes closed, I felt around for my toothbrush, my pinky finger making contact with the bristles. I grabbed its handle and groped around for the faucet. *Got it.* I ran my toothbrush under the warm water and somehow managed to squeeze out toothpaste. The taste of fresh mint overwhelmed my mouth, awakening my senses.

I had just cracked open one eye when my uncle turned on the light without warning. "Ahhhh!" I cried, covering my eyes with my free hand.

"Rise and shine, Lucy," he chirped.

"Morning, Uncle Tom," I answered through the foam in my mouth. I blinked a few times to adjust to the light and rinsed out my mouth.

"Tough morning already, huh?" he asked, nodding at my toothbrush.

I wondered what he was talking about. I looked down at my hand and realized that I had just brushed my teeth with my aunt's toothbrush. "EWW!" I exclaimed, spitting what was left of the toothpaste.

"Ew is right, Lucy. If you needed a new toothbrush you just had to ask," he laughed, nudging me in the shoulder. I took a swig of mouthwash and gargled a few times, completely ignoring him. "The damage has already been done, Lucy," he giggled, reaching across for his own toothbrush. I spat out the mouthwash and stuck my tongue out at him through the mirror. He shook his head. "We leave in less than thirty. Alright, kiddo?"

"Yeah, yeah, yeah," I said, faking a huff before turning and heading to my room.

On our way to the airport, the sun was barely rising over the horizon. *It should be illegal to be up this early,* I thought, yawning.

As I looked out the passenger side window of my uncle's SUV, cars already filled the streets. I wondered if that would be me someday, an early riser with a daily commute.

"Excited to go back home?" my uncle asked, bringing me back from my daze.

"Kinda," I answered, thinking about my family.

"Yeah, I bet your mom and dad missed you," he added, turning into the airport.

I sat up straight and smiled. *My avenue to adventure*, I thought, taking a deep breath.

My uncle pulled up to the curb, popped open the trunk, and handed me my luggage. Excitement swarmed my stomach as I knew that I would once again see the world from a bird's-eye view.

"Oh, and here you go. Don't forget about these," he said, unloading two additional huge suitcases.

My aunt's sister-in-law was expecting a newborn baby, so my aunt offered to send her all her old maternity clothes and a gazillion baby outfits through me. I sighed, wondering how in the world I would manage to make it to the check in kiosk.

"Have a safe trip, kiddo," he added, pulling me in for a hug I smiled brightly and wrapped my arms around his waist.

"Thank you so much for everything, I had a blast!" I said, pulling away.

"The pleasure was all ours, Lucy. Now go, otherwise I'll be late for work."

I slipped on my backpack and somehow managed to grab hold of the three handles. I took a step towards the entrance and paused.

"Make sure you kiss Sean and Caroline for me," I said, smiling from over my shoulder.

My uncle smiled softly. "I will, don't worry," he nodded.

I grinned, turned around, and headed into the airport.

Once inside, I stood in line for what felt like an eternity to check in all of my bags and to get my boarding passes. *Gate G14.* I passed through security with flying colors and followed the signs to my gate. I took a seat and waited for my zone to be called. It was all too familiar, and I was both eager and excited for what was to come.

My zone number was called, my boarding pass was scanned, and I headed inside the tunnel for my seat, *25D.* I walked down the tiny aisle and smiled tenderly at seat 17A. I wondered how Deborah was doing. There was no doubt in my mind that after having met Walker, she had found the turmoil of her trip oh so worth it.

I stopped in front of *25D* and confirmed it with my boarding pass. *Yup, that's it,* I thought, taking off my backpack. I took the seat next to the window and slid my backpack underneath the seat. I watched as people in the aisle filled up the empty spaces around me.

A quick glance at my watch revealed we were scheduled to depart in eight minutes. *Hmm, maybe I'll get lucky this time around and have both seats for my own,* I thought, planning on stretching my legs.

The flight attendant took a head count as I wiggled anxiously in my seat. With three minutes left, a man huffed and puffed his way down the aisle. Somehow, I knew he was my seatmate.

"Excuse me, I'm sorry, thank you, excuse me," he repeated, collapsing next to me. "Phew!" he exhaled, his breath slapping me in the face like a brick wall. "I can't believe I made it!" he said, wiping the sweat from his forehead.

I forced a smile and turned towards the window to inhale some uncontaminated air. I took a deep breath, but it was cut short at the unforgiving smell of his body odor. I gagged. I couldn't believe my luck.

"Hi, I'm Jim," he stated.

I forced my nostrils closed and immediately became a mouth breather. Slowly, I turned to face him. He had his hand held up for me to shake. I took it.

"Lucy," I answered, and for the second time, I forced a smile.

At any other given time, I would have politely initiated small talk. However—for the sake of survival—I was willing to be the "antisocial teenage girl."

Jim smiled, reclaimed his hand, and struggled to buckle his seatbelt. Ignoring him and his rancid breath, I leaned my head against my seat and closed my eyes. Though I wanted nothing more than to look through my window, I knew that it would have to wait.

Through the takeoff process, I drifted off a couple of times, half listening as people settled down around me. Gradually, the plane leveled as we reached cruising altitude. Still unwilling to make small talk with my seatmate, I opted to keep my eyes shut just a little longer.

"Anything to drink?"

I tensed up for a second, trying to decipher whom the flight attendant was addressing.

"Ehh, yes. Coffee please."

I had recognized the man's voice. It was Jim's.

Multiple thoughts crossed my mind. *Should I open my eyes? Do I want something? Am I hungry? Is it worth dealing with his bad breath? Wait, he ordered coffee. Maybe that will help mask his mouth's disgusting scent.*

On impulse, I opened my eyes and addressed the flight attendant's back.

"Excuse me?" I stated loudly, hoping that she would hear.

From the corner of my eye, Jim smiled before tapping her on the shoulder.

"Yes, sweetie, how may I help you?"

"Could I have a glass of apple juice and a bag of pretzels, please?"

"Sure," she smiled, handing me my items.

I thanked her, took a sip of my apple juice and plastered my face against the window. There wasn't a single cloud in the sky and I could see as far as my eyes would let me. I was in awe.

There was a slurp next to my ear. I glanced at Jim; he was holding up a newspaper with his left hand while mechanically returning his cup to its designated groove.

As I was about to toss a handful of pretzels in my mouth, Jim—engulfed in his reading—misjudged the placement of his cup, spilling his coffee onto my lap. I gasped, and he panicked.

"Oh no! I am so sorry!"

He grabbed his napkin and began absentmindedly sponging out the hot liquid from my lap. I froze in shock as his hands touched my thighs.

"It's fine, I got it," I said, wishing his hands away.

Immediately realizing what he had done, Jim turned red, apologized, and got up. Luckily for me, I had been wearing jeans, which served as a barrier from the hot coffee.

Moments later, Jim returned with a handful of napkins, this time handing them all to me. I forced a smile, thanked him and cleaned my lap as best as I could. *This has already been one heck of a day.*

A few hours later, the captain came on, announcing that we were preparing for landing. *Thank you Jesus!* I thought, ready to get out of the plane. *This landing could not have come soon enough.*

The airplane's wheels screeched as they made contact with the runway. It was only a matter of minutes before I would be able to stretch my legs.

As soon as the seatbelt sign turned off, Jim got up, grabbed his suitcase, and stepped out into the aisle.

"I hope that the rest of your trip goes smoother than this morning . . . and again, I am so sorry for that," he said, nodding at my coffee stained pants.

I smiled, accepted his apology, and wished him all the best. I followed him out of the plane and into the tunnel.

Once in the airport, Jim turned left, disappearing into the crowd while I turned right, never to cross paths again.

I had planned to spend my two-hour layover roaming around in the Hamilton Airport. But first, I headed to the bathroom. With a wet napkin, I locked myself into one of the stalls and scrubbed the coffee stain out of my jeans.

After five diligent minutes, my pants had semi returned to their original state. I came out of the stall and checked my image in the mirror. I laughed in disbelief. The coffee stain was gone, but for the second time that day, I looked as if I had peed my pants. I took a deep breath. *At least it'll dry.*

It was nearly noon by the time I walked out of the bathroom, and I was starving. I grabbed a freshly brewed cup of French Vanilla cappuccino and a chocolate glazed doughnut from a coffee shop nearby, and headed towards my gate. I took a seat facing the empty kiosk and took a bite of my doughnut. *Pure bliss.*

I was enjoying my solitude, when a lady with two teenagers took a seat right in front of me. The entire boarding area was vacant, and I wondered why in the world they had chosen to awkwardly sit directly across from me. The lady, who I assumed was the mom, looked in her early 40's, the girl looked as if she was my age, while the boy appeared a little older.

Suddenly, the mom smiled at me, and I realized that I had been blatantly staring. I blushed and looked away.

I was trying my best to seem interested in anything other than them, but I couldn't help sneaking a glance once in a while. I mean, they had chosen to sit right in front of me after all.

The gate agent's voice came over the intercom and the girl my age looked at me and smiled. Unable to ignore them for a second time, I smiled back genuinely and shuffled around for my boarding pass. I located my zone number, waited for it to be called and headed into the plane.

Unlike my previous flights, this time my assigned seat was on the aisle. I looked past the overweight gentleman seated to my right, and I envied him. Unlike me, he would have the luxury of the window view.

The cabin crew began their safety demonstration, and the plane started moving on the runway. *Four more hours,* I thought, glancing at my watch. I couldn't wait to be reunited with my family.

The plane took a slight left turn and then stopped. At first, I didn't think much about it, but after fifteen minutes of standing still, my patience began wearing thin.

"Do you have any idea what's going on?" I asked, tapping my seatmate's shoulder.

"No, I'm not sure. There must be some air traffic or something," he said, before looking out the window.

Ding.

"Ladies and gentlemen, this is your Captain speaking. We are encountering difficulties in communicating with the main tower. We are foreseeing a twenty-five-minute delay, but as soon as we get this issue resolved, we'll be on our way. We apologize for the inconvenience, and we ask that you remain patient with your seatbelt securely fastened. We will let you know when we have more information. Thank you."

A few sighs were heard throughout the plane, and I felt the same. I looked at my watch; it was 1:33 p.m.

When 1:58 rolled around, there was still no update from the cockpit. The plane's engine had been running on reserve mode, disallowing the luxury of air conditioning. In no time, the muggy cabin was making everyone sweat.

The overweight gentleman to my right was fanning himself with the safety information card. The lady in front of me shed her last layer, and I could do nothing other than roll up the bottom of my jeans.

Ding.

"Ladies and gentlemen, the issue hasn't yet been resolved and we are foreseeing an additional twenty-minute delay. Thank you for your patience."

Are you kidding me? Another twenty minutes in this sauna, I thought, wiping the sweat from my brow. *This isn't happening.*

Passengers groaned while I looked around for a distraction. *Come on, give me something*, I thought, looking down the aisle.

Then, as if he heard me, a man got up from his seat, popped open the overhead bin and started shuffling in his bag. I watched carefully, wondering what he was looking for. *A snack? His headphones? Deodorant maybe?*

Suddenly, a glass bottle of cologne slipped out of his bag. I gasped, watching helplessly, as it came crashing down on an elderly gentleman's head. He cursed and grabbed his injured scalp. When he pulled his hand back, it was covered in blood. Someone yelled out for help and the flight attendant instantly rushed to his side, trying her best to control the situation.

"Sir, sir, can you hear me?" The old man's hand collapsed on his lap. "Jeanette, call the paramedics!" she ordered, addressing the other attendant. Jeanette disappeared to the front of the plane while her coworker applied pressure on the wound with gauze.

Since we were still on the ground, it took no time for the ambulance to arrive. The vehicle's sirens were screaming for dear life when I heard a loud *bang* coming from the front. *Good, they're here*, I thought, concerned for the old man's safety.

The airplane's door popped open and in came two paramedics. One took the man's vital signs while the other assessed the severity of the cut.

Ding.

"Ladies and gentlemen, I understand that there has been a minor accident in the main cabin and we kindly ask that you remain seated with your seatbelt fastened. Thank you."

Better late than never, I thought, rolling my eyes at the useless announcement.

I watched as one of the paramedics cleaned and dressed the old man's wound while the other jotted down notes. They forced the old man onto his feet to assess his stability. *He looks fine to me*, I thought watching him walk up and down the aisle.

The paramedics seemed to share my opinion. The three men shook hands and the old man returned to his seat.

Ding.

"Ladies and gentlemen, due to the unfortunate accident, it is company policy and standard procedure for us to file a report. This process takes about twenty minutes. Thank you for your patience."

I shook my head in disbelief. *Be careful what you wish for*, I thought, recalling my earlier request. I glanced at my watch; it was 3:15.

As the heat on the plane escalated, it was a miracle that no one else fainted. Though my patience was wearing thin, I knew that I had a choice to make. I could either sit and gripe at this uncontrollable situation or laugh at its absurdity.

I knew from experience that a bright, genuine smile was deemed contagious, and I decided to hand them out like candy. I looked at the lady across the aisle from me and smiled. She smiled from her eyes before taking a deep breath. *One for one*, I thought, happy with my decision. I looked to my right at my seatmate who was still fanning himself with the safety information card and, I grinned. He looked at me for a split-second before reciprocating.

I had grown to embrace the body odor that lingered within the plane, and I had come to accept the severity of my sweat stains. I was proud of my decision to see the glass half full, while just moments ago I had deemed it half empty.

I heard a toddler laugh, and suddenly, I saw the situation for what it actually was. Everything that had happened was out of my control, and yet, I had allowed its repercussions to take an emotional toll on me. I had felt anger, resentment, and anxiousness all due to an unforeseen delay. At the sound of a *ding,* my carefree demeanor had changed to one of bitterness and frustration, welcoming all sorts of negativity. I groaned and for a brief moment was ashamed of myself.

I had subconsciously chosen to worsen my mood rather than better it with my attitude and for that, I shook my head in regret.

I thought about my last hour and a half and imagined what I could have done differently. *Well, I guess it doesn't matter anymore. What matters now is how I choose to react from this moment on,* I reasoned, finally learning the lesson.

CHAPTER 3

LIGHTS OUT

D*ing.*

"Ladies and gentlemen, in order to maintain your safety as well as the safety of our crew, I would like to inform you that no other plane will be cleared for takeoff at this time." The captain paused. "There has been some sort of electrical outage impairing communication between all airborne flights and ground reception. Unfortunately, no definite time has been given as to when this issue will be resolved. Due to these unforeseen circumstances, we are left with no other choice than to disembark the plane. We ask that you calmly retrieve the items you've placed in the overhead bin. Your checked luggage will be dispensed at Carousel number 3. Thanks again for your patience and understanding."

I couldn't believe what I was hearing. They had kept us captive in this hotbox for nearly three hours only to tell us that they still couldn't take us home. I laughed in disbelief.

I stepped out of the plane and took a deep breath. Instead of inhaling the lingering smell of body odor, I was hit by dense humidity and stuffiness. The farther I stepped into the airport, the worse it got.

In an attempt to keep a positive attitude, I decided to occupy my mind.

"Carousel 3, Carousel 3," I whispered.

A crowd had formed around the still conveyor belt, and I wondered how long it would take them to bring out our bags. I looked around at a few familiar faces, trying my best to ignore the sweat beads that were forming on my forehead.

How much longer until this thing starts moving? I thought impatiently. Then it dawned on me: there was no electricity!

At that moment, I noticed two men in reflective vests hauling carts full of luggage. One by one, they unloaded the bags while passengers buzzed around them like flies. I sighed. *It's not like scrambling to retrieve your bag will get you out of here any faster.*

I waited patiently for the crowd to dissipate before hauling my bag out of the pile. I pulled up my retractable handle and began walking away from the chaos when a sudden thought crossed my mind: *my aunt's suitcases.* I felt my temperature rise even higher.

Why? I cried internally, *Whyyyyy?*

I looked at the mass of suitcases, trying to recall which ones my uncle had handed me. *One was green . . . or was it gray? I know it was a dark color . . . no, it has to be dark green . . . I think. Maybe the other one was gray?* Staring at the pile of different colors, I no longer knew where to begin.

After reading countless luggage tags, I was finally able to collect both of my aunt's suitcases— forest green and navy blue.

Seeing me walk down the corridor towards the customer service desk must have been quite the scene. I had hooked my aunt's suitcases together, hauling them with my right hand while my left hand lugged an oversized suitcase of its own.

By the time I had reached the customer service desk, a long line had formed in front of the two clerks who were trying their best to tame sweaty, impatient passengers. I huffed and puffed at the back of the queue, my mouth feeling like the Sahara Desert. *Water. I need to get water.* I clacked my dry tongue onto the roof of my mouth in an attempt to stimulate saliva, but it yielded nothing. It too needed water.

I slowly inched my way forward. *I don't know how much longer I can take this,* I thought, staring ahead.

For the last 10 minutes the only thing that had kept me somewhat entertained was the odd couple standing in front of me.

The lady, who I presumed was the wife, was leaning on her husband, whispering relentlessly. I wondered how he could tolerate her in such heat. Halfway engaged, the man nodded once or twice. They, just like the rest of us, were suffering from this intense heat.

The man's bald head was glistening from sweat. His light blue shirt was soaked all the way through to a shade of navy. As I watched him some more, I couldn't help but notice his back hair curling at the neck. I stared, repulsed, unable to turn away. With each head motion, the hairs on his collar swayed sluggishly as if tiny burdens were weighing them down. Both disgusted and fascinated, I wondered how on earth he had gone bald.

"Miss. Excuse me, miss."

I had been so engrossed by the man's neck that I hadn't even noticed the woman addressing me. Her hair was in a tight bun, and she wore a Canadian Air pin on her shirt. She held something out in front of her.

"Ice Cream!" I said, probably louder than I should have.

She laughed. "Yes, we are handing them out for free. Would you care to have one?"

It was like she had been sent from heaven.

"Oh my gosh, yes! Thank you so much. You have no idea how thirsty I am," I said, grabbing the wrapper. Immediately, I bit my tongue. *Of course she knows how thirsty you are . . . she's standing in the same heat as you!* I cringed.

"You are so welcome," she stated, before moving on to the couple in front of me.

Immediately, I began unraveling the wrapper. The ice cream was already melting and the cone's edge was a bit soggy, but I didn't care. All that mattered was that it was cold and refreshing. I sunk my teeth into it and slurped the running milk. I could hear my taste buds rejoicing. I took another bite. *Mmm . . . so good.*

I swallowed my last bite and licked my lips, making sure that no drop was wasted. I couldn't remember the last time an ice cream cone had tasted that good.

I looked at the line. We had surprisingly made progress. *Only seven people left ahead of me.*

"Next, please," the customer service rep called out.

A lady with two teenagers pulled away from the desk with a piece of paper in hand. I had heard that they were giving hotel vouchers to compensate passengers and hoped that despite my age, I would be granted one, too.

For a brief moment, the lady made eye contact with me and smiled. I recognized her immediately. She and her children were the ones who had awkwardly sat in front of me in that empty terminal.

Slowly, she began closing the distance between us, and for a moment I wondered if she had smiled at someone else. I quickly glanced over my shoulder, but no one seemed engaged in her stare. Finally, she stopped a few feet before me.

"Bonjour," she stated in a horrible French accent.

"Bonjour," I replied, nodding.

"Ehh es tu, voyage emm sol. Emm reste avec nous a hotel?"

What the heck are you saying to me? I thought, trying my best to decode the phrase she had just butchered. My lack of immediate response sparked her to try again.

Though I knew how to speak French, why she had assumed that it was my first language, I had no idea. Wanting to spare her from further embarrassment, I cut her off.

"Do you speak English?"

She let out a sigh of relief. "Yes!" she said excitedly. She resumed her earlier questions, but this time in English.

"Are you traveling alone? Do you want to stay with us in the hotel?"

My heart pounded. In any other circumstance, I would have said no. My mom had always warned me to beware of strangers, but this situation was different. Here I was at fourteen, stranded in another province, half a country away from my home. Unable to drive and with no cellphone, I felt helpless.

Going with what I thought was rational, I followed my gut instinct. I opened my mouth and noticed the lady's kids smiling brightly behind her. I took a quick glance at the line.

"Sure!" I exclaimed, relieved.

"Great! Come with us."

I stepped away from the line and wondered if I had made a mistake.

The lady introduced herself. "I'm Janie. This is my son, David, and my daughter, Lindsey," she added.

"I'm Lucy, Lucy Sawyer," I stated, shaking their hands. "Thank you so much for inviting me to stay with you guys. I was standing in line like everyone else, but honestly, I had no idea what I was going to do. This is only my second time flying."

"Second time flying?" David asked. "Man, I can't imagine being your age and traveling by myself. How old are you? Sixteen, seventeen?" I laughed and shook my head.

"No, I just turned fourteen two months ago."

Janie's jaw nearly hit the ground. "What?!" she exclaimed. "I thought for sure you were at least sixteen. You look Lindsey's age and she's just about to turn seventeen."

I blushed, unsure of what to say next. It wasn't the first time that someone thought I looked a little older than my actual age.

"So, do your parents know what's happening?"

My parents! I thought, slightly panicking. I hadn't given them a second thought. I glanced at my watch; it was nearly 5:30 p.m. *I should have landed by now.*

Feeling like an irresponsible child, I answered, "No, actually. Ever since we left the plane, I've been in line for my suitcases and then in line for the vouchers."

"I see. And I assume you don't have a cellphone?"

"No, I don't."

"Hmm, I would let you use mine, but it's dead now. I've spent the last hour calling around trying to figure out what's going on."

"And . . . did you find anything?"

"Not really, only that there's been a huge power outage, but you already knew that," she winked, smiling at me.

I was at ease. These people were merely strangers, but I already felt comfortable around them.

"Alright, listen. You see that line over there?" I nodded. "Okay, well those people are waiting their turn for the phone. I'm not quite sure how it's still working, but at this point that's your best bet at contacting your parents."

"Okay, thank you." I sighed with relief. "I can only imagine how anxious my mom is at this point."

I turned and grabbed my suitcases when suddenly, David's voice spoke out.

"Lucy, don't worry about your luggage. We'll bring them over. Just get yourself in line before it gets even longer," he said, reaching for my handles.

"Are you sure? They're heavy."

He laughed, and I forced a meek smile. I couldn't believe I had just said that to a guy who was much older than me.

"Thank you," I mumbled, before turning around and jogging towards the line.

After a few minutes, I slowly but surely made my way up to the front of the line. I could already hear my mother's panicked voice at the other end and I shuddered, wiping the sweat from my forehead.

"Next please." The lady's voice came from behind the counter. Calmly, she smiled brightly before handing me the receiver.

"Phone number?" she asked.

Out of habit, I began reciting my home phone number but stopped myself mid way. The lady's finger hovered a few seconds above the number pad before glancing up at me.

"Is everything okay, miss?"

"Ehh . . . yes, but I just realized that my parents wouldn't be at home. I live two hours away from the airport, and they were coming to pick me up."

She quickly glanced at the line behind me before addressing me again.

"Is there another phone number I can dial for you?"

"Yes, just one second," I said, taking off my backpack. "Actually, you can let this guy go before me while I find what I'm looking for."

The gentleman behind me smiled, and I stepped off to the side.

Where is it? Where is it? I wondered, shuffling through the front pocket of my backpack. My mom had insisted on giving me a family friend's phone number. She lived near the airport, and we were intending on spending the night at her house. I knew that's where my parents would be.

Janie was by my side like a mother hen. "Is everything okay?" She had already taken me under her wing.

"Ah ha!" I exclaimed, unfolding the crumpled piece of paper. "I knew it was in there," I added, relieved.

Janie's shoulder dropped as she exhaled sharply. She too had shared my tension.

"Are you ready, miss?" I smiled, grabbed the receiver and handed her the piece of paper.

Ring, ring, ring. The phone rang for so long that I was beginning to lose hope when, all of a sudden, I heard a *click* at the other end of the line.

"Hello?" It was Sue, our family friend.

"Hi, Sue. It's Lucy."

"Oh, thank goodness! Where are you?"

"I'm in the Hamilton Airport. No other plane is flying out today because of some sort of blackout."

"Yeah, it's all over the news," she stated. "We were waiting at the airport when they told us the situation. Of course, your mom panicked and you know her, she wanted to stay, so I convinced your dad to bring me back home just in case you would call."

"Sue, it's really not that bad. It's not like my plane crashed or anything."

"Ha! It's your mother you need to say that to. Speaking of the devil, they just pulled up. Hang on, I'll get her on the line."

I quickly looked behind me. Somehow, the line had tripled since the last time I had seen it, each person anxiously waiting their turn to use the phone. I didn't know it was possible, but at that moment I began sweating more.

My mother's panicked voice came on the receiver. "LUCY! My God! Thank goodness you're okay."

"Mom, relax, I'm fine. There is some sort of blackout out here, making it impossible to have any communication with the towers. We can't fly out today."

"I know. That's what they told us. On top of that, it's all over the news. Are you okay? What are you going to do?"

"Mom, I'm fine. Everything will work out. I met this lady. Her name is Janie, and I'll be staying with her and her kids."

"Wait, what?" Immediately, she went into overprotective mode. "Janie? Janie who?"

I covered the mouthpiece with my hand and asked Janie for her last name.

"Hello? Lucy? Janie who?"

"Janie Mitchell, Mom. I'll be staying with her."

"Oh no you are NOT!" she screamed into the phone. "I don't know anything about this woman! Lucy, you're only fourteen for God's sake!"

"I know, but what else am I supposed to do?"

"You stay right where you are, and we'll drive up to get you!" *Did she really just say that?* I thought.

I could hear Sue in the background trying to rationalize with my mother.

"Mom . . . Mom," I called, trying to bring her attention back to me. "Mom!"

"WHAT?" she barked.

I took a deep breath and exhaled sharply.

"Mom, you're more than fifteen hours away. By the time you get here, I'll already be reassigned and probably landing in Moncton. Look, there is a long line of people here waiting their turn, and I've already overspent my time limit."

"Time limit? Wait, what?"

"I have to go, Mom. I'll call you back later."

"Lucy, don't you dare hang up this phone . . . "

"Bye, Mom. Love you."

She was still speaking as I handed the receiver over to the lady behind the desk. I smiled shyly at her, turned around, nodded apologetically at the gentleman behind me and pulled myself out of the line.

"Is everything okay?" Lindsey asked, once her mom and I had rejoined them.

"Yeah, my mom is just going crazy with worry, that's all. But who can blame her, right?"

"I sure can't," Janie said, shaking her head. "I can't even imagine."

CHAPTER 4

A RIDE TO REMEMBER

We stepped out of the airport, and though the air outside was just as warm and humid, at least there was a breeze.

"So, what's the plan now?" I asked Janie, relieved that I had someone to depend on.

"Well, we have a hotel voucher, and the agent told me that taxis were lining up out here to bring us to our destination. So now we wait."

"How far is this hotel?" David asked, fanning himself with his shirt.

"Obviously, we weren't the first ones in line," she said taking a deep breath. "In fact, we weren't even the first flight to receive vouchers. The agent told me that our hotel is about twenty-five to thirty minutes from here." She wiped the sweat from her brow. "This is home stretch, guys. We are so close," she added, waving down a cab.

I was ecstatic when the yellow car came to a halt in front of us. For one, I no longer had to haul my ginormous suitcases behind me; and two, I was eager at the thought of air conditioning.

"Hrrello," the man said, stepping out of his car. I noticed that his first language wasn't English.

"Hi," Janie said brightly. "We need to get to Hotel Omena."

The man frowned for a second before forcing a smile. "Yes, yes. I know. No problem," he said, opening the trunk.

For some reason, the tone in his voice made me uneasy, but I brushed it off. All that mattered was that he could bring us to our destination.

The cab driver attempted to fit as many suitcases as he could in the back of his compact car. I knew this task would be impossible. Between the four of us, we had six large suitcases, one carry-on, and three backpacks. I clenched my teeth, angry that my aunt had pawned those suitcases off on me.

After ten minutes of persistent shuffling and rearranging, the cab driver was left with no other choice.

"Sorry, but some will go on lap."

The man's shirt was soaked with sweat, and his body odor was pungent. I opted to breathe through my mouth. Janie took the front passenger seat and straddled her carry-on suitcase along with her son's backpack. I took the window seat behind her, Lindsey took the middle, and David sat behind the driver. My backpack sat in between my legs, and on my lap was one of my aunt's massive suitcases. Unfortunately, David was facing the same torture. Lindsey, on the other hand, held her backpack to her chest, her right leg bearing some of my suitcase's weight and her left one doing the same for David. All of a sudden, the "home stretch" didn't seem so close after all.

The cab's engine rattled as it pulled away from the curb. *Please God, don't let this ride be more than 30 minutes,* I prayed. But apparently, God had other plans.

Fifteen minutes in, and I could no longer bear the awkward silence. The cab driver had not said one word to us. I suspected it was due to his limited English.

His skin was the color of cinnamon, his hair was dark, almost black, and he had a scruffy beard. He wore a type of hat that I had seldom seen before, and I wondered how he could stand it in this heat. Sweat dripped from his temples, and it suddenly dawned on me that he hadn't extended the courtesy of turning on the air conditioning. Instead, both front windows were wide open, and the back windows, which were child-locked, were cracked no more than three inches.

My right leg had gone numb, and my left leg wasn't far behind. Silently, I prayed again. *God, please let us be close. Oh, and please let there be cold water at the hotel. Thank you.* I had barely finished my thought when the car came to a halt. I looked out the window and noticed graffiti painted across what looked like an old, abandoned building. I wondered where we were. I leaned over, looked out the front window, and immediately my heart sank. The line of cars sitting ahead of us was appalling.

What the heck? What could it be? A car accident? A road block? Then it hit me. *No electricity*. No power meant no traffic lights, and no traffic lights meant that all major intersections had become four-way stops. I wanted to cry. I looked at Lindsey who shared my anguish. Plus, to make matters worse, air was no longer circulating in the car, making my yearning for water even greater. There was no way we'd be getting to the hotel in the agent's estimated time.

Slowly but surely, car by car, we made our way to the front until finally it was our turn to proceed. We took a right. It seemed to me as if we were headed away from civilization, but I had no clue where we were. We had no other choice than to trust this cab driver.

Beeep-Chrrrrrr. The driver's radio sounded from the front, and our cab driver answered it in a foreign language. He spoke quickly, almost in a panic, and just as soon as he had answered it, he hung up. I didn't recognize the language, but my guess was that it was Arabic of some sort. Whatever had been said seemed to have flustered our cab driver, who was now taking abrupt turns and breaking harshly. I looked at my watch; we had left the airport 45 minutes ago. In disbelief, I nudged Lindsey with my elbow and showed her my watch. She winced, shook her head, and nudged her brother so she could silently relay the news. It was as if no one dared to talk.

We took a sharp turn and the weight of my suitcase shifted entirely onto my left leg. I bit my lip to refrain from making any sound. Wide-eyed, I leaned forward past Lindsey and looked at David. He glared at me and shook his head. He was about to mouth something to me when an uneasy feeling grew in the pit of my stomach. Through the rearview mirror, the cab driver was staring right at me. I don't know why, but his brown eyes paired with his dark bushy eyebrows made me uncomfortable. *Does this guy even know where he's going?* I thought, nervously facing the side window. I no longer dared looking up.

Beeep-Chrrrrr. The cab driver snatched up his radio and began speaking again. This time, the conversation was a little longer. I could tell he was angry. I assumed that the person on the other end of the line was his boss. Finally, with a snarl, he hung up.

We came to a stop sign, and the way he braked was as if we were about to rear-end another car. Almost an hour had passed, and I was over this roller coaster. I glanced at the meter. So far, we owed him $76. I couldn't believe it. I prayed that the taxi voucher would cover it, but deep down I knew that we had well exceeded the allotted amount.

We merged onto what seemed to be another highway, and I began seeing civilization again. With the warm breeze now circulating full force through the car, I felt a sense of relief. Surely we were close.

A few minutes passed before we took an off-ramp, and immediately the car came to an abrupt halt. I peered forward and saw a line of cars ahead of us. I sighed. We just had to be patient. The meter was at $94.

I looked out the window, and suddenly, it was like déjà vu. The worn-down building, the graffiti, we had been here before. Shocked, I sat up quickly in my seat. *What just happened?* This guy was either lost, or he was taking us on a deliberate detour. I panicked but didn't want to alarm the others. I looked in the rearview mirror, and the cab driver was squinting at me. I didn't know what was happening, but we needed to get out of there.

Then, the radio sounded, and the driver picked it up in a fury. He was no longer trying to tame his anger and let the person on the receiving end of the monitor have it. When all was said and done, he slammed the receiver down and exhaled sharply.

I looked at Lindsey and David, who seemed just as anxious, and I wondered how Janie was holding up. I leaned to my right and caught a glimpse of her death grip on the armrest. Her fingertips were white, which told me all I needed to know.

Beeep-Chrrrrrr. There it was, that sound again, and I knew all too well what was bound to happen next. He picked up the receiver, kept it short and slammed it shut. Not thirty seconds later it sounded again, and this time our cab driver turned off the monitor completely. The silence in the car was deafening. We took a left, and I opened my mouth to speak, but Janie's voice took over.

"Are we almost there?" she asked sternly.

The cab driver glared at her before answering, "Yes. Got lost and boss no help. I shut him up." The way he had spoken was as if he had silenced the man for good.

My anxiousness grew deeper as I glanced at the meter, $117. I rubbed my temples while trying to devise some sort of plan. Nothing. I couldn't think of anything. The only idea I had was to fake the need to pee, forcing him to stop, which would allow us to make a break for it. And then what? We would be stranded in a foreign town and Crazy Cabby would hold our luggage hostage? No. That wouldn't work.

Janie spoke again. "With all due respect sir, how much more time before we get there? This is getting ridiculous."

This time, the driver didn't bother looking at her. His hands were gripping the steering wheel, and he was hunched over.

"Fifteen minutes," he growled.

Lindsey's jaw dropped, and I blinked rapidly, trying to wake myself up from this terrible nightmare. *Another fifteen minutes*?! I thought in disbelief. *That's how long it should have taken us from the airport!* I sighed, knowing that no matter what, we were at this man's mercy.

I stared at my watch like a hawk, counting down the minutes. I knew that if we didn't get there soon, I would erupt. My mouth was dry and my empty stomach was eating itself. Not to mention that I was borderline motion sick by now. I glanced at the meter; $125. This was absurd.

At the fifteen-minute mark, as the meter hit $157, we pulled into a parking lot and came to yet another abrupt halt. The Hotel Omena sign was barely visible due to lack of electricity, but I didn't care. I had never been so happy to see a hotel in my entire life. I pushed open my door and shoved my suitcase to the ground. *Freedom at last*!

I swung my legs out of the car and stepped out. To my surprise, they buckled under my weight and I found myself lying flat on top of my suitcase.

"Lucy! Are you okay?" Lindsey asked, rushing to my side.

"Yeah, I'm fine. I think my legs just gave out. It was weird."

I sat up and saw the suitcase's imprint on my legs. Then it hit me: pins and needles. "Ow, ow, ow," I mumbled, massaging my legs. The pain was nearly unbearable, but still, I needed to retrieve my stuff. With Lindsey's help and with the aid of the car door, I was able to stand on my own two feet. "*Ow, ow, ow,*" I whined again, stomping my feet.

By this time, all the suitcases were out of the car, and the cab driver was staring at Janie with a "*Are you going to pay me?"* type of look. She had the voucher in her hand, and I knew that she wasn't willing to give him anything else.

"Kids, grab your suitcases and go inside," she ordered.

Without a peep, the three of us struggled to quickly haul our possessions into the lobby. Shortly after, Janie joined us. Thankfully, we never saw the cabby again.

CHAPTER 5

BRICKS IN MY SUITCASE

Heaven, oh sweet heaven! Pure bliss. Water sent from God himself. Praise you! I was on my fifth cup, but still parched. *Thank you so much! This is delicious. The best thing I've ever tasted*, I thought, pouring myself another cup. The sound of the air bubbles coming from the water dispenser tank emanated like a chorus of angels, and at that moment I couldn't have been more grateful.

Janie was talking to the front desk lady, and due to the lack of electricity, the check-in process was taking twice as long.

"What a crazy ride, huh?" Lindsey stated, still in disbelief.

"Crazy doesn't even begin to cover it," David chimed.

"Yeah, and I'm just glad I didn't have to go through that by myself," I shuddered.

"Yeah, I am too," David agreed.

My stomach growled louder than it had in the car, and I blushed.

"I'm hungry too," Lindsey admitted. She looked at her watch and gasped. "Well no freaking wonder, it's a quarter past eight!"

Partly in disbelief, I glanced at my watch to make sure it wasn't a joke. She wasn't kidding.

"Unbelievable," David growled. "This has been one hell of a day."

"You got that right, son," Janie chimed, finally joining us. "Okay guys, the voucher is valid for one free room with two queen beds, but don't worry, they'll bring us an additional cot," she said, winking at me. "Oh, and these are for you," she added, handing us each a flashlight.

The sun was slowly setting and with no electricity, it was only a matter of time before the place turned dark.

"Alright kids, we're on the 5th floor, room 525," Janie said, grabbing her carry-on.

"Sweet," I said, gathering my suitcases.

I was leading the way towards the elevator when I stopped dead in my tracks. No electricity meant no elevator. No elevator meant stairs. And stairs meant one heck of a climb with my three suitcases all the way to the 5th floor. For the second time that day, I wanted to cry.

All of us groaned in despair as Janie opened the door to the staircase. We were met by complete and utter darkness. Our four lights flicked on weakly as we prepared for our climb. Knowing that I couldn't possibly haul three ginormous suitcases up five flights by myself, I opted to leave one behind for a second trip. That thought alone made me want to weep, but I was determined not to complain. The last thing I wanted was for this gracious family to consider me spoiled and rotten. I strapped two of my suitcases together as I had done at the airport, shoved my flashlight into my mouth and began my climb.

I hauled, tugged, pulled, and dragged my burden behind me, nonstop until the second floor. When my suitcase's rear wheels made full contact with the level floor, I hunched over, snatched the flashlight out of my mouth, and panted for air. I could barely hear the others over the sound of my heavy breathing and wondered if they were struggling as much as I was.

Lindsey's light vanished around the corner and in fear of falling too far behind, I resumed my torture.

By the fourth floor, my teeth had dented the handle of my cheap flashlight, and I was drenched with sweat. "One more floor, twenty more steps," I whispered, "you can do this." One by one, with everything I had left in me, I conquered the final climb to the fifth floor.

"We made it," Lindsey puffed.

"We sure did!" I agreed.

Janie led the way and we walked in a single file, shining our lights on every door number until we reached room 525. She pulled out the room key, placed it in the lock and pushed open the door. I was ecstatic. David opened the curtains and the light that entered the room was barely more than that of a few lit candles.

"Guys, I suggest that each of us shower and then we can all go out in search for some food. What do you think?" Janie asked.

"Oh my God, yes!" Lindsey said, clapping her hands. "Shotgun!" Before anyone else could protest, she had already unzipped her suitcase and was fishing out some fresh clothes. "I'll be quick," she smiled, turning on her flashlight and disappearing into the bathroom.

"So, Lucy, it's been quite the eventful day and we haven't had much time to chat. Tell us a little about yourself," Janie said with a smile.

Still unsure of the sleeping arrangements and not daring to soil the clean bed, I pulled the chair from under the computer desk and collapsed.

"Well, there isn't much to the story really," I said honestly. "I have an aunt who lives in British Columbia and she had invited me to come spend the summer with her and her family. I was there for a whole month and a half, and now I'm on my way back home. Well, at least trying to get there," I laughed.

Janie smiled and shook her head. "Well, I have to say that you are the bravest fourteen-year-old I have ever met," she praised. I blushed.

"Well, I have to say that you guys are the bravest family I've ever met. I don't know many people who would volunteer to take a complete stranger under their wings."

"True, but there was something about the way you smiled at us when we sat in front of you during our connection. You seemed honest and genuine. When I saw you standing in line by yourself, my motherly instincts just took over," she admitted.

"Well, whatever it was, I am very thankful to have met you guys and that I'm in good hands."

At that moment, Lindsey came out of the bathroom looking like a new person and instantly, David sprung up.

"I'm next!" Not thirty seconds later, he was in the bathroom.

"Honestly, that was the best shower I've ever had," Lindsey raved.

"Well don't rub it in," her mom laughed. I giggled. They truly were the best family to be stranded with.

Lindsey and Janie conversed while I mentally picked out what I was going to wear. I looked at my suitcase, trying to recall what was in it, when it suddenly dawned on me: one was missing. *Oh no!* I screamed internally. I had left it downstairs.

My heart sank, and I contemplated leaving the thing behind, giving it away or deliberately forgetting about it. The mere thought of having to haul one more burden up five flights of stairs was nearly unbearable.

I wish Dad was here, I thought. But I knew that no matter how much I prayed, fussed or griped, that suitcase was my obligation and it was my responsibility to take care of it. I sighed loudly and got up.

"I just remembered, I left one of my suitcases downstairs. I'm going to go get it and I'll be right back," I said, forcing a smile.

"Okay, do you need help?" Janie asked.

"No, I think I got it. But thank you for the offer," I said, faking a smile before turning around and disappearing into the hallway.

A part of me couldn't believe I had turned down the help. A simple "Yes, that would be great, thank you," could have divided that burden in half, but instead I had chosen to suffer all by myself. *It's not their load to carry*, I rationalized. *They've already been beyond gracious, and you need to carry out your sentence.*

My aunt had entrusted me with two big suitcases, thinking that her generosity was an act of kindness. Instead, her gesture had turned my journey into a punishment, one that was binding, and I was forced against my will to see it through.

I reached the ground floor and pushed the staircase door open with a sigh. My aunt's green suitcase was standing tall next to one of the lobby plants, just where I had left it. I resentfully grabbed the handle and let the weight of the bag fall onto the palm of my hand before dragging it bitterly behind me. I shoved the end of my flashlight in my mouth, pulled open the staircase door and began my climb.

By the time I reached the second floor, I was already out of breath. *How is this even possible?* I thought, irritated. The fact that I had earlier carried two oversized suitcases nonstop to the second floor blew my mind. I yanked the flashlight out of my mouth and wiped it with my shirt.

"Why are you making this so difficult on me?" I growled, kicking the bottom of the bag. Resentfully, I bit the end of my flashlight once more and began hauling it up another flight of stairs. The sweating was back with a vengeance and the salty droplets stung my eyes

I stopped again on the third floor to catch my breath and wipe my brow. "I'm barely halfway," I whispered, my voice brittle, before pressing forward. I huffed, puffed, struggled and hauled, unable to believe how heavy this suitcase was. It was as if it had doubled in weight, and for a moment, I wondered if someone had mischievously put a brick in it.

I hate you, I thought pausing for the third time. *Why couldn't you be smaller and lighter?*

With each progressing step came a surge of anger. By the time I had reached the fourth floor, I was raging. It no longer mattered that I was one floor away from my destination. It no longer mattered that I was so close from my goal. It no longer mattered that I had covered so much ground. Instead, all I could think about was how unfair this had been.

I despised the cards I had been dealt. I cursed at the suitcase and bashed its side, hating it for all it was and for all the pain it had caused me. Exhausted, I sat at the bottom of the staircase, twenty steps from my goal, pinned down by self-pity. The light from my flashlight flickered. *Yeah, go ahead . . . die. I dare you. Make my burden heavier.*

To my surprise, it didn't. Instead, the light seemed to shine brighter, and I found myself inhaling deeply through my nose. My chest rose while I held the air inside of my lungs captive. When I could no longer bear the burning sensation, I exhaled slowly. I could feel my body cooling-off and my anger slowly subsiding. I switched the flashlight to my left hand and examined the suitcase for damage. Nothing. It was as good as new.

My mind drifted to the suitcase's content, and I imagined the joy on my pregnant aunt's face as she pulled out outfit after outfit. I smiled. Then, the whole scene turned cold as I imagined the disappointment on her face when I told her that I had purposefully left the suitcases behind because they were an inconvenience. In that dark staircase, on the fourth floor, I felt ashamed.

I was ashamed at the selfishness that I had allowed to lurk inside of me, ashamed that I had let anger poison my veins, and ashamed that I had permitted negativity to overpower my thoughts. I sighed in disbelief. Even though I had let this whole thing get out of proportion, I was glad that I had regained perspective. Partially relieved and feeling somewhat lighter, I stood up and loosened my shoulders.

"You and me, we're going to conquer this last floor and I promise you'll make it home," I said, just before placing the flashlight in between my teeth. I bent over, one hand gripping the handle and the other slipping underneath the suitcase. *One, two, three, and up.* I took a step forward, amazed and shocked at how light the luggage felt. *Nineteen more steps to go*, I thought, cracking a smile. *Eighteen, seventeen, sixteen . . .* I felt as if I was covering ground effortlessly, gliding up the stairs. And it was at that moment that I realized that in some way, I had been the one who had placed the bricks inside the bag; that all along, my attitude and thoughts had altered the weight of my burden.

CHAPTER 6

NOT ALL THINGS ARE AS THEY APPEAR

I emerged out of the shower feeling completely refreshed, with a new perspective. As I slipped into my clothes, it blew my mind to think that this whole adventure had started less than fifteen hours ago. Once dressed, I bent forward to towel dry my hair and a loud gurgling sound came from my stomach reminding me that it was empty. I was famished. I pulled my hair back into a ponytail and stepped out of the bathroom.

"Feeling better?" Lindsey asked, with a knowing smile.

"Better?! Ha! I feel brand new!" I exclaimed.

"I don't know about you guys, but I'm so hungry I could eat a horse right now," David stated, in a more serious tone. It was as if he had read my mind, and silently I thanked him.

"Well, I think we all are, honey. Let's go venture out to see what we can find," Janie said, standing up.

I slipped on my shoes, grabbed my wallet and located my flashlight as David opened the door to the hallway.

It wasn't until we walked out into the parking lot that I found myself missing the constant glow of streetlights. Apart from the glimmer of headlights from the nearby highway, we were totally engulfed by darkness. Even the moon seemed to have taken the night off, hiding behind dense clouds. I clicked on my flashlight, more grateful than ever for our complimentary gift.

Though the night had cooled off slightly, the concrete still emitted heat from the sun's relentless rays. It, too, had fallen victim to its unyielding heat.

We covered ground in search of food, our eyes peeled for the slightest sign of life. At this point, we were open to anything so long as it would help tame our hungry stomachs.

We walked a little further before coming across a gas station, and I couldn't help but cheer in excitement at the dim light. The front door was propped open, and there was a man standing behind the checkout counter. *Hallelujah,* I thought, picking up the pace.

"I'm already not a big fan of gas stations in broad daylight," Lindsey whispered, "but at night, with no electricity, there's no telling what goes on in there."

"Oh don't be ridiculous, we're going to be fine," David said, shaking his head.

"He's right. You can't think like that, Lindsey," I said chuckling. "Besides, I've personally never been more excited in my life at the thought of chocolate bars and chips!"

Janie knocked on the propped opened door. "Excuse me," she said, catching the man's attention.

"Well, hello there! Welcome to the Blackout Corner Store," he chuckled. "How may I help you?"

Lindsey let out a faint sigh of relief.

"Well," Janie smiled, "for starters, you are open, right?"

"As long as this keeps working," he said, nodding at the small generator.

"Great, because I have three hungry kids, and I can't even remember the last time we ate."

The man inspected us silently from head to toe. The way he had frowned made me wonder what was going through his mind. Janie caught the look on his face and spoke again.

"We're not homeless or anything," she laughed. "I guess I should have worded my sentence more carefully. We were traveling home by plane and Hamilton was only supposed to be a layover, but with this whole blackout thing, we've had an eventful day with little to no food."

"Oh." The man nodded, color flushing his cheeks. "Please forgive me, it's just that in a situation like this where light is minimal, I have to take extra precaution. And, if I'm being honest, for a minute there I was suspicious," he admitted shamefully. "Already my wife thinks I'm crazy for keeping the store open, and the last thing I want is for her to be right in saying that I would just be welcoming trouble."

"I totally understand, and I guarantee we won't be any trouble at all," she assured him.

They continued their conversation while the three of us wandered through the aisles. I had finally settled on a granola bar and a box of Ritz crackers when I heard Janie exclaim, "Excellent!"

"Hey guys," she said, grabbing a candy bar, "apparently, there's a Subway a few minutes down the road, and according to Chip here, it should still be open. Are we up for it?"

The thought of sinking my teeth into a freshly made sandwich made my mouth water, and my stomach growled louder. Embarrassed, I quickly brought a hand to it and laughed.

"Umm. I think that's a yes from me," I stated, walking up to the register.

"You don't have to tell me twice," Lindsey said, following behind me.

"Oh my God, yes!" David said, ripping open his bag of chips.

"Then it's settled," Janie stated, smiling brightly.

After settling our dues with Chip, we found ourselves on the empty street once again consumed by darkness.

"Do you really think that Subway will be open, Mom?" David asked, crumpling his empty bag of chips.

"I sure do hope so, honey. I sure do hope so."

"Well it better b— Eeek! What was that?!" Lindsey screeched, hopping behind her brother. Her sudden scream had made my heart sink to my stomach and immediately my palms became clammy.

"I don't know, but I heard it too," David stated stiffly.

Forced to be the brave one, Janie began scanning the area with her light. Tree, shrubbery, tree, more shrubbery, shining eyes!

"What IS that?!" Lindsey screamed, now gripping her brother's shirt.

"I'm not sure," her mom whispered.

Through a dense bush, something with unblinking eyes stood nearly three feet off the ground.

A branch cracked, and I swung my flashlight beam in its direction. My breathing became shallow, and I could hear my heart pounding in my ears. I had uncovered a second pair of eyes.

"Guys . . . " I whispered. The silence of the night was now deafening, and for a moment I felt like a trapped prey. "Guys . . . " I whispered again, this time loud enough to be heard.

"I see it too," David whispered, taking a step back.

"Eeeekkkk!" Lindsey was the first one to take off running. The sound of her footsteps, paired with her screams, sparked the rest of us to follow suit. We quickly bolted the distance of three telephone poles before finally coming to a halt. With her hands on her knees, Lindsey was panting harder than normal.

"What—the—heck—was—that?" she asked in between breaths.

"I have no idea . . . and don't act like you actually care to find out," David accused, shaking his head. "By the way you took off running, you—"

"Hey! I believe you came in second, just behind me. Don't pretend like you were big and brave, tough guy. Plus—"

Lindsey and David were cut short by Janie, who had finally managed to catch her breath only to lose it again to laughter.

"Mom, would you care to share what on earth there is to laugh about in a time like this?" Lindsey asked, a little dumbfounded.

Janie's laugh grew louder as she attempted to point at her source of laughter: me.

"Ehh, I don't get it?" David shrugged his shoulders.

Did she just point at me? Surely that was a mistake. What did I do? I was at a loss for words when Janie pointed in my direction again. Tears of laughter were now streaming down her cheeks, and I could feel the blood rushing into mine.

"Rips," she managed to blurt out between breaths.

Oh my God! Did my jeans rip? I thought, checking my pants. The thought of that alone had me sweating for the millionth time that day. *Nope, nothing here. Nope, nothing there,* I thought, patting my rear end. Lindsey flashed her light to the front of my jeans.

Still overtaken by laughter, Janie managed to shake her head "no" before stating it again, "Ripts."

What is it? I don't get it!

"Ritz!" Lindsey exclaimed, pointing at the box in my hand.

"And what in God's name is so darn funny about that?" David asked, slightly annoyed.

I looked down and all the crackers within my newly opened box were gone. I shed what little light my flashlight emitted just behind Janie, and just as I had suspected, there lay a piece of my snack. I took a step forward, shined my light a little further and spotted another piece. I erupted into laughter. It wasn't long before Lindsey and David caught on, joining in on our belly laugh.

After a few minutes, Janie finally caught her breath. "Oh my goodness, that was so funny," she stated, wiping a tear from her eye. "Here I am, one minute afraid for everyone's safety, and then the next I am running for my life pummeled by Ritz crackers."

I shook my head in disbelief while sponging tears from the corner of my eyes. "Well, on a positive note, guys," I said, inspecting the bottom of my box and dangling my granola bar, "good thing I bought more than one snack."

Lindsey giggled, and David's stomach growled. "You know, we could have all munched on your Ritz crackers, Lucy, but I'm glad you decided to attack my mom and feed the beasts instead," he mocked.

"Yeah, yeah, yeah . . . better the crackers than us, that's for sure," I said, tearing my wrapper. "Plus, we all needed a bit of comic relief," I added, sinking my teeth into the bar.

"Hey guys, is that what I think it is?" David asked, excitedly.

"Well, would you look at that," Janie exclaimed, grinning.

I looked ahead at the faint light and blinked a few times just to make sure that my eyes weren't deceiving me.

"Subway!" Lindsey squealed, jumping up and down.

The thought of biting into a freshly made sandwich had my taste buds dancing in anticipation.

"Let's go, guys! Especially now that Lucy doesn't have anything to throw at you, Mom," David snickered, before taking off. The three of us giggled and followed behind him.

It took us a total of five minutes to reach Subway's parking lot. Despite being in a commercial area, the darkness made me feel as if we were the last people left on earth. The Subway sign was plugged into a portable generator, and a small red extension cable kept the front door cracked.

"Is there even anyone in there?" Lindsey asked, peering through the window. The light inside the building was faint, but it was still clear to see that there was no one in sight.

"Hello?" Janie called, opening the front door.

The jangling sound of the entrance bell pierced through the sound of the generator.

"Hello?" David called louder, but there was no one in sight. David puffed his chest, in one final attempt to call out, when a woman appeared from behind a swinging door.

"I thought I heard something," she smiled, reaching for a new pair of plastic gloves. "What can I get for you?" We all sighed in relief.

Lindsey ordered first. While waiting for my turn, I looked around in this dimly lit sandwich place. Something was off, yet I couldn't put my finger on it. *Is it the color of the walls? The dim light? How we got here? This unbearable heat?* I was racking my brain, staring aimlessly at the chopped-up veggies when I noticed that all of them looked dull. My heart sank. I looked over my left shoulder at the little extension cable, and I wanted to scream. No electricity meant using generators; generators meant limited refrigerators; and lack of refrigeration meant no crisp veggies. And just like that, my hope for a fresh sandwich wilted away like that lettuce.

I slid in the booth, the back of my legs sticking to the green faux leather, and stared at my lifeless sandwich. *Am I the only one feeling this way? Should I say something*? I was about to open my mouth when a thought crossed my mind, *You haven't even tried it yet, why are you so quick to judge?*

Why was I so quick to judge? While the Mitchells seemed to be enjoying their food, I had lost my appetite. I took a sip of my lukewarm water and in fear of being called out for not eating, I sunk my teeth into my turkey sandwich. *Hmm, not as bad as I feared*, I thought, staring at the whole-wheat bread.

"You know, this isn't the prettiest looking sandwich," David mumbled, his mouth half full, "but I sure am glad we have something other than chips and chocolate to hold us over."

"You're right, it may not be the prettiest, but remember we are often deceived by our eyes," Janie stated, putting her sandwich down on a napkin.

The tone in her voice suggested that there was more to her statement; and all of a sudden, my entire focus was on her.

"If you can learn something from this life, I wish it to be that you understand that not all things are as they appear. Often, we take what we look at for face value without actually taking the time to seek the truth. Our eyes deceive us by creating images that our mind or heart is blind to. This causes us to act on impulse, enticing us to make decisions solely based on external appearances rather than facts. We need to go beyond that instinct by learning to look and listen at the same time. What did your eyes see? What does your heart tell you? Are you hearing the voice inside your head? Are you listening to it? Sometimes what seems absurd to others may make total sense to you and we need to learn not to give in to the social pressure. Don't ignore your senses; stay in tune with them, trust them, and the world will open to you. It's amazing what we can experience once we truly learn to see."

Each word echoed in my head. I understood her point so clearly that my seemingly irrational decision in trusting complete strangers was now making total sense. I had, despite my mother's panic, opted to trust my gut. Unknowingly, I had ignored the societal norm, seen past the immediate picture and chosen to listen to something other than fear.

CHAPTER 7

THE FORGOTTEN CALL

The door clanged behind us as we stepped out of Subway and into the night. The air was still thick and humid, but I was finally beginning to cool off.

"Do you think we'll be able to fly out tomorrow, Mom?" Lindsey asked, kicking a pebble.

"I wish I could answer for sure, sweetheart, but there really is no telling," she answered, putting her arm around her daughter. Lindsey sighed before kicking another pebble. "Oh come on, it's not so bad. What happened to your sense of adventure?" Lindsey glared at her mom.

"I think I sweated it all out," she answered sternly, keeping a straight face.

Silence hung in the air for a few seconds before David laughed. No longer able to maintain her poker face, Lindsey chuckled, joining the rest of us in a laugh.

"I hate to say it, but that was a good one," David admitted, shaking his head.

"I just couldn't pass it up," Lindsey replied, gloating in the moment.

I was still smiling when I noticed the silhouette of the gas station we had visited earlier. As we got closer, it was clear that the owner had returned to his family. The front door was now closed and the glowing light from inside had disappeared, making the whole place look asleep. I yawned.

"I'm right there with you, Lucy." Lindsey patted my shoulder. "What time is it anyway?"

I looked at my watch and my jaw dropped. It was 10:55 p.m. A surge of thoughts invaded my mind. *How can it be so late? Oh dear God, my mother! She's probably pacing back and forth, worried to death. She's going to kill me. There's nothing I could have done differently though . . . it's not my fault there is no electricity. Nope, she's still going to kill me.*

"Lucy, are you okay?" Lindsey asked, placing her hand on my shoulder. I flinched.

"It's 10:55 p.m. I'm sorry, I am just panicking because the last time I spoke to my mom was over six hours ago, and there is no doubt in my mind that she's far surpassed the point of being worried. Plus, they're an hour ahead of us . . . she probably thinks I've been kidnapped."

I automatically picked up the pace. Everyone followed, while Janie did her best to comfort me.

"I can definitely see where you're coming from, Lucy, but it'll be fine, honey. As soon as we get back to the hotel, we'll find a way to get in touch with her and if you think it'll help, I'll talk to her as well, okay?"

My heart was pounding harshly in my ears, but I nodded and forced a smile anyway. Despite her calm and reassuring demeanor, I could tell by Janie's tone that she could relate. There was no doubt; she had momentarily stepped into my mother's shoes.

I reached the hotel parking lot, sweating profusely. *How could I have been so selfish? Why didn't I think about calling sooner? How could I have been so self-absorbed?* The more I questioned my lack of judgment, the more anxious I became.

I was ahead of everyone and within yards of the front door, when a deep male voice stopped me dead in my tracks.

"Is everything okay?" he asked, flashing a light directly at my face.

I covered my eyes and gasped in surprise. Despite the sweat, chills traveled up and down my spine.

"Miss, is everything okay?" he asked again, sternly.

Still blinded by the sudden brightness, I answered. "Yes, everything is fine. You just scared the heck out of me."

By this point, Janie, Lindsey, and David had walked up behind me and were now receiving the same bright light treatment.

"Hello sir, my name is Janie Mitchell and we are all temporary guests of this hotel," Janie stated calmly, shielding the bright light with her hand.

"You said Janie Mitchell?" he asked, shining his light on a stack of paper. "Would you mind confirming your room number for me, please?"

"Sure, not a problem. Our room number is 525."

The security guard flipped through a couple of pages before stopping. "Thank you. As you all know, most hotel security runs on electricity and since that's out for now, we are forced to take special precautions in terms of who walks in and out of this hotel, especially at this hour. We don't want any unwelcomed guests."

"No, we completely understand, and I'm glad that you guys are doing that." Janie smiled in relief. "Thank you."

"Of course. Safety is my first priority. Have a good night." He opened the door, letting us past him.

The receptionist at the front desk greeted us with a smile, but I had only one idea in mind; calling my mother.

"Good evening, how was your night?" she asked.

"It was good, thank you," I muttered all in one breath before zooming past her and into the staircase.

I was about halfway up the third flight of stairs when my name echoed off the walls. I paused for a second, trying to hear past the sound of my panting, and then I heard it again.

"Lucy!" David's voice called out.

"Yes?" I answered, walking down two steps.

"Come back! My mom has her phone ready for you."

I raced down the stairs.

"Janie, I thought your phone was dead?" I panted.

"It was, but when we checked in, I asked if there was any way they could partially get it charged. Luckily, this nice lady had an external charger with an adapter that fit my phone. So here," she said, handing me her cell. I was so relieved that I felt like hugging her. Immediately, I recalled the numbers to my calling card and dialed them in a hurry.

"Thank you for dialing Canada Prime, please enter the phone number, including the area code, of the person you are trying to reach."

I was pressing each number carefully when suddenly, my heart dropped even further in my stomach. *She's not at home.* I was dialing my home phone number for the second time that day, forgetting once again that my mom wasn't even there.

"What's wrong?" Janie asked scanning my face. "Oh, wait . . . the other phone number," she sighed. Despite our limited source of light, I caught a flash of empathy crossing her face and her motherly instincts kicked in. "Alright, everybody take a deep breath. Let's all go up to the room so that Lucy can call her parents. David, since you have the key, lead the way."

Without any objection, David stepped past the receptionist and into the stairwell.

"Let's go, Lucy," Janie said urging me forward.

That was all it took for me to scurry into the staircase, climbing the steps two by two.

"Thank you for dialing Canada Prime, please enter the phone number, including the area code, of the person you are trying to reach."

Janie read the numbers off the crumbled paper, and I held my breath in anticipation. The phone had barely rung once when I heard a *click* followed by a gasp of relief.

"Lucy?! Oh, thank God you're okay!" my mom said at the other end of the line. "Sweetie, how are you?"

Not the response I was expecting, I thought, relieved at her reaction. "I am good, Mom, how are you?"

I had barely spoken out the last word when my mom jumped full force on her rant. "Do you have ANY idea how stressed out we were? I was worried sick about you, do you hear me?! And do you have ANY freaking idea of how long I've been waiting by this phone praying to God for it to ring? Well, let me just—"

No longer able to stand her scolding, I gently removed the phone from my ear, forced a smile and shrugged my shoulders at Janie, who was sitting directly across from me. She smiled back and for some reason, I felt a little better.

"Mom, Mom," I said, into the receiver, trying to put an end to her outburst. "Mom," I called again, but no such luck. "Caryn!" At the sound of her name, my mom took a sharp breath. "Mom, I'm sorry I had you worried sick. But in my defense, I'm caught in a blackout, and I don't have a cellphone. Landlines are only working in certain areas and to be quite honest, we've had a heck of a hard time getting to our hotel. On top of that, we've spent the last two hours searching for a place that sold something to eat other than chips and candy."

"That is no excuse! You still could have found the time to call me, Lucy. The last time I heard from you was almost nine hours ago. You just turned fourteen, for God's sake!"

I could hear my dad in the background trying to calm her down, but despite his attempt, it seemed only to add more fuel to her fire.

"I know, Mom. You're right," I stated earnestly, knowing that there was no point in further pleading my case.

"Now tell me where you are, starting with who. And if you hang up on me like you did earlier today, I swear to—"

"I am currently staying at Hotel Omena, which is about 30 minutes from the airport," I cut her off. I could no longer bear the lecture nor tolerate the embarrassment. "I am staying with a lady named Janie Mitchell and her two children, Lindsey and David. They have been great, Mom. Had it not been for them, who knows where I would have ended up . . . " *Gosh Lucy, why would you say that?* I thought, biting my tongue.

I was racking my brain for something else to say when Janie caught my attention. She pointed to the phone in my hand and pointed to herself. *Hallelujah!* I thought, sighing in relief.

"Mom, would you like to speak with Janie?" My mom had been silent for a few seconds, and for a moment, I wondered if she was still on the other end of the line. "Mom? Hello?"

"I would love to," she said, clearing her throat. Surprisingly, she sounded calm and rational. I handed the phone to Janie like it was a hot potato.

"Hi Mrs. Sawyer . . . Caryn, sure. Yes, that's right Janie, Mitchell . . . Of course, no problem at all. I totally understand. I am from Laurencetown and I was traveling back with my two children when I came across your daughter. I just figured that if one of mine were caught in a situation like this that I would prefer for them not to be alone, you know . . . No, no, she's been no trouble at all. She's been a pleasure, really. Absolutely, my cell number is 555-212-3243, but I just want to remind you that we have limited source of power, and I'm not sure how much more battery life my cellphone will have. Yes, I will make a conscious effort to remind her. You are most welcome. Likewise, it was a pleasure speaking with you, and I look forward to meeting you as well." Janie smiled and handed me the phone with a slight wink.

"Hi, Mom."

"Hi, Lucy. Well, she seems very nice, honey."

"Yeah, she really is. In fact, they all are," I stated shyly.

"You do realize how lucky you are to have come across them, right? Janie is like your guardian angel." I blushed, knowing that my mom was right.

"Yes, she is. I am extremely lucky," I agreed.

"Okay, well it's late, so go get some rest and CALL ME TOMORROW."

"I will, I promise."

"Okay, well I'm glad you are safe and in good hands. Good night, honey. I love you and keep me posted."

"I love you too, Mom. I'll talk to you tomorrow. Bye." *Click.*

I let out a sigh of relief and Janie did the same.

"You have a good mom, you know? She loves you very much."

"Yeah, I know. It's just hard because she just gets so . . . how can I say this . . . passionate." Janie laughed and wrapped her arm around my shoulder.

"I know it's hard to imagine right now, but in a few weeks, we'll all be laughing about this. Don't forget, you are a very sweet and special kid, Lucy. Not to mention brave, but hey, you don't need a stranger to tell you that." Janie smiled and gave me a gentle squeeze.

At that moment, the child in me wanted to hug her. But for some reason, I froze. There was so much I didn't understand. It would have been so easy for her to brush me off, pass me by, or ignore me. I wasn't her responsibility and yet she felt compelled to approach me. *What possesses a person to do that? Why me?* I had so many unanswered questions, and yet here I was, safe among this family. *How could that be?*

My head was spinning with thoughts when my mother's words pierced through them all: *guardian angel.* Those two words echoed in my mind and all of a sudden, my questions had vanished. Just as Janie pulled away, I wrapped my arms around her waist and squeezed her tight.

"Thank you. Thank you so much for everything," I choked out.

"I wouldn't have it any other way, Lucy." She patted me softly on the back.

A knock on the door made David rush to the peephole. "Mom, I can't see properly but I think it may be people from the front desk."

"Oh, that must be the cot I asked for. You can open it."

David opened the door, shining his light on the people standing in the hallway.

"Hi, I think you guys requested a cot, right?" one of them panted. I felt bad for them, knowing all too well the challenge of having no electricity and climbing to the 5th floor.

"Yes, that's us." David stood aside as the men pushed the cot in. "If you could just put it right there, that would be great. Thank you so much."

"No problem at all. Have a good night."

As the door closed behind them, I felt a surge of excitement at the thought of finally lying down. It had been an extremely long day for all of us and this was like a prize at the finish line.

CHAPTER 8

UNEXPECTED LESSON

I woke up to a beam of light peeking through a slit in the blinds. I shaded my eyes and wondered what I was doing in a place surrounded by floral walls. As the seconds ticked by, I recalled the events of the last 24 hours.

Whoa, did all of that actually happen? I thought, stretching. I propped myself up onto my elbows and looked around the room. Lindsey, David and Janie were all still sound asleep. I glanced at my watch; it was 7:17 a.m. *How am I even awake right now*? I thought, lying back down. Just as soon as my head hit the pillow, I found the answer. *It's because of you.* I groaned, blinded once again by the beam of light. *I guess it's hard to cover all the cracks at night when it's just as dark inside as it is outside,* I thought, pulling the sheet over my head.

"Lucy. Lucy, wake up sweetie."

Janie's soft voice brought me out of my slumber. I pulled the covers from my head and regretted it. The room was so bright that I squinted my eyes and rolled onto my stomach, turning my back to the window. I rubbed my eyes and reopened them, this time, slowly, allowing myself to adjust to the bright light.

"Wake up, honey," Janie said, addressing David. "It's time to get up."

"What time is it anyway?" he grumbled, burying his face into his pillow.

"It's eight. I know you're tired, but we need to get ready and be at the airport by noon. At least that's what the agent told us yesterday. So, chop chop!"

Lindsey sprang out of bed. "Guys, I think we're finally going home today, I can feel it!"

Despite enjoying the Mitchell's company, I couldn't help but share her excitement.

"Yes, I have a good feeling about it too, but let's make sure we aren't late to the airport. I wouldn't want, after all this, for us to miss our flight," Janie added, zipping up her suitcase.

The air in the room was thick and warm. As I waited my turn for the bathroom, I glanced out the window at the dark pavement. I could see heat waves radiating from the street, and already, I wasn't looking forward to another sweat-filled day.

Since the electricity was still out, I took two trips to manage the load of my suitcases. This time however, I let gravity do most of the work. Letting my suitcases lead the way, step after step, *thud* after *thud,* we made our way down the staircase. By the end of my second trip, I hoped I would never have to repeat this process again.

"There she is!" Janie grinned as I stepped into the lobby. "They are offering us free breakfast."

"What?! You mean we won't have to run for our lives or actually step out in this heat in search for food?" I said sarcastically.

"Nope. Nor will I risk the chance of getting attacked by flying crackers," she winked.

"Well, that's true," I giggled. "Plus, free breakfast is like music to my ears."

Janie laughed and shook her head. "That's exactly what Lindsey said."

I placed my third suitcase in the pile next to the others and followed Janie into the breakfast room. With no electricity, our choices were limited to overripe fruit, bread, bagels, muffins, jam, peanut butter, warm cream cheese, and dry cereal. I grabbed a tray and took my place in line.

As I inched forward towards the food, I overheard two elderly ladies gossiping about the airport.

"Pfft, they told us to be there around noon, but I bet a thousand dollars that they'll just have to turn us back around."

"Now Clarisse, you need to be more positive. If they asked us to come back, it's because they genuinely think they're going to be able to send us off today."

"Yeah, well, I doubt it. I still think they needed to be more prepared for this type of crisis. Take this place for instance—it's twenty miles from the actual airport; they had limited generators; our room had no air conditioning; and I nearly suffocated from the heat in my sleep."

"I was in that room too, you know, and it really wasn't that bad," the other lady responded calmly.

"Speak for yourself, Evelyn. I barely made it out alive, and now this 'breakfast' will have us starving within the hour. I mean look at this . . . no toaster, no microwave, not even coffee!"

"Clarisse, you need to take a deep breath and be thankful that you have food. I'm sure these people are doing the best they can with what they have."

"Yeah, well, in my opinion, this isn't good enough. Whatever 'bug' infiltrated the electrical system should have been removed by now, and I should already be home," she sniffed, slapping a piece of limp bread on her plate.

Clarisse's friend shook her head and took a deep breath. I could tell she was doing her best to maintain her composure.

As we made our way forward, Clarisse did nothing but gripe and complain. She filled her cup with lukewarm water, coated her bread with peanut butter and reached for the jam spreader. To her disgust, it was covered with sticky fruit residue. She quickly dropped it onto the counter and reached for a napkin. Rather than wiping off the substance, as it is designed to do, the white tissue stuck to her hand.

"Ugh!" she screamed.

The more she tried, the worse it got. When half the napkin was shredded onto her palm, Clarisse took a different approach. Cursing under her breath, she reached into Evelyn's tray, snagged her napkin, and dunked it into her water cup. She began rubbing the wet ball of mush onto her hand, and to her delight, it was working. In search of another napkin, Clarisse looked past her friend and quickly snatched the one from underneath my silverware. I looked at her wide-eyed, taken aback by her rudeness.

"Stupid place, stupid people, stupid blackout, stupid breakfast . . . " she grumbled, dunking my napkin into her water.

As fate would have it, Clarisse dropped my wet napkin onto the floor. On her way to retrieve it, her elbow made contact with her tray sitting precariously on the counter, sending her freshly buttered bread colliding directly onto her back. She stiffened. Still hunched over, she took a deep breath and began straightening herself out. I watched as gravity took its toll, sending the plate crashing to the ground.

The sight of the bread clinging onto her white shirt had me fighting tears of laughter. Clarisse stood erect and slowly turned towards her friend. With pursed lips and flared nostrils, she deliberately reached behind herself, scraped the piece of bread off her back, and in one swift motion, flung it down onto Evelyn's tray. No longer able to contain herself, Evelyn erupted into laughter. Clarisse's eyes narrowed and blood flushed her cheeks.

"Get your suitcase and call a cab. We're getting the hell out of this place!" she hissed.

Before Evelyn could even say a word, Clarisse turned sharply onto her heels and stormed out of the room.

Laughing, Evelyn bent down reaching for the fallen tray. I mirrored her, picking up the plate.

"Oh, thank you dear, but to be completely honest, neither of us should have to pick up after that old crank," she said, wiping a tear from her eye. "I keep telling her that what goes around comes around and whatever she puts out in the world comes right back to her, but that old fart never listens to me. I've known this woman for over seventy years, and it just amazes me how—despite all of her life lessons— she just won't change. I guess to you youngins this would be called *Karma*." Evelyn sighed and shook her head. "I'll tell you one thing though, if I hadn't personally seen our birth certificates, I would have bet my life that one of us was adopted."

"You two are related?!" I blurted out.

Evelyn smiled tenderly and nodded her head. "Flesh and blood my dear. Can you believe it? She's my older sister."

I blushed. "I . . . eh . . . I didn't mean to—"

Evelyn laughed.

"Don't worry sweetie, I would have said the same thing if I were in your shoes. But . . . " she said, resting her hand on the counter, "I do take comfort in knowing that despite the fact that we are kindred, we are two polar opposites." I smiled shyly and nodded my head. "I've learned a lot from her though," Evelyn continued, picking up the empty water cup. "Yup, a lot about what NOT to do."

For some reason, I couldn't help but soak in the wisdom and grace of this petite, white haired lady.

"You see, there is always a lesson to be learned or an opportunity to show kindness, my dear. No matter the circumstance. And often, a situation is neither good nor bad, but our thinking and how we respond to it makes it so," she said, pinching my cheek.

She headed towards the trash can and started to leave the room as I racked my brain for something to say.

"Wait!" I blurted, just as she was stepping out of the room.

Evelyn turned around and waited for me.

I grabbed a muffin and a piece of fruit. "Just because your sister ruined her breakfast, it doesn't mean you need to pass up on yours." I handed her the muffin. "And just in case she changes her mind, here," I added, offering her the banana. Evelyn smiled warmly.

"Sweetheart, kindness and compassion are qualities that are hard to come by. Don't ever lose them. Time is too precious and life too beautiful for us to grow bitter and hard like my sister. Thank you." Evelyn squeezed my arm in a grandmotherly fashion and whispered, "You truly do reap what you sow." With one last loving smile, she turned on her heels and disappeared into the lobby.

By the time I sat down with my breakfast, Lindsey and David were almost done with theirs. As I sank my teeth into my bagel, I thought about Evelyn's words, '*You truly do reap what you sow.*' The more I thought about it, the more I had questions. *Why did she say that? What does it truly mean?*

A tap on the shoulder brought me back to reality.

"Hellooo? Earth to Lucy . . . are you okay? I just called your name twice, but you didn't answer. You know, there are more interesting things in life than your bagel, right?" David laughed, standing up from the table.

"Oh, sorry, it must be this wonderful, warm slab of cream cheese," I replied jokingly, "which . . . I am absolutely thankful for, by the way," I added with a grin.

"Ha! Yeah, I hear you there. But, as I was saying, want me to grab you something to go? I'm not sure how much food they'll have at the airport so I'm stocking up just in case."

"Sure. Whatever you're having is fine with me."

I scanned the table, and to my surprise, everyone's plate was empty but mine. Feeling pressed for time, I took a heaping bite of my breakfast and gulped it down with warm water.

"What are you trying to do?" Lindsey laughed. "Win an eating contest?" Caught red-handed, blood rushed to my cheeks. "Who are you competing against anyway?" she added, staring at the empty plates.

"Ehh . . . my . . . self?" I took another bite and peered at my watch.

"Ohhh, a competition against time; that's always fun," she winked. "Go, Lucy, go!"

Now fully committed, I swallowed my last bite and raised my hands up in the air as if I was the victor. Both Janie and Lindsey clapped, and I took a bow. I was beyond thankful for them.

"Alright guys, are we all ready?" Janie asked, looking at her watch.

"Yes, I beat my record, so I think my job here is done," I answered, pushing myself away from the table. Lindsey giggled and shook her head. "But seriously, thank you guys for waiting," I added shyly.

"No problem at all. To be fair, it was actually pretty funny seeing you stuff half a bagel into your mouth." She laughed. "Oh, and for the record, we still have plenty of time."

I smiled sheepishly, stood up, and followed her into the lobby.

It was about nine thirty when our airport shuttle pulled up to the lobby entrance. All of us were antsy to get going. In less than three minutes, we had hauled our suitcases out into the scorching heat. I had never been more thankful at the sight of a minivan.

"Good morning, Mitchell party of four, correct?" our driver said, looking at his clipboard.

"Yes, that would be us," Janie answered eagerly.

"Great. My name is Mike and I'll be responsible for bringing you guys to the airport today," he grinned. "I'll take the biggest suitcase first, please," he added, reaching for one of mine.

"I'm thankful we don't have to carry those on our lap this time," David whispered.

"Ha! If that's not a sign that this is going to be a good day, I don't know what is!" I sighed in relief.

After trial and error, we were able to fit all of our suitcases, backpacks included, into the back of the van.

"We're all set!" Mike wiped the sweat from his forehead.

Janie hopped into the front seat, and the rest of us sat in the back of the van.

Since the car's engine was still off, sweat immediately trickled down my temples. I looked through the window at Mike who was jotting down notes on his clipboard. As the temperature rose, I silently pleaded for him to hurry. Seconds turned into minutes, and finally the driver's side door opened.

"I'm sorry about the wait, guys. I just had one last section to fill out before we could get going, but now we're all set," he smiled, sticking the key in the ignition. The engine roared, and I felt the cool, unadulterated bliss blowing onto my face. I closed my eyes. *Air conditioning, at last!* It had never felt so good.

As my hair danced happily in the breeze, I was swept away by my own thoughts. *Hopefully, we get to go home today. I know Mom and Dad have been worried sick, which reminds me that I need to call them once I get to the airport. Hopefully Janie's phone still has battery, or I can use Canadian Air's landline if it works. What caused all of this anyway? What set it off? Why is it taking them so long to reinstate power?*

Our car came to an abrupt halt. I peered out the front window and stared at the long line of slow moving cars.

"One thing is for sure," Mike said scratching the back of his head, "we never know how dependent we are on something until it's gone." *I couldn't agree more,* I thought, recalling my struggle in the staircase. "But don't worry, as soon as we get past this intersection, we'll be less than fifteen minutes away from the airport."

"Did he just say what I think he just said?" Lindsey whispered, leaning into me.

We had been in the car for a total of twelve minutes, and already we were halfway to our destination.

"This is what yesterday's ride should have been like," David added, shaking his head.

As we slowly made our way up the line, I thought, *It only took one bad experience for us to appreciate the good.* The more those words lingered in my head, the more I found that they made sense. There were so many things before this trip that I took for granted. Because of this blackout, thousands of people's lives, including mine, were turned into complete chaos. It made me realize just how dependent we are on certain things and how hectic life can get once those privileges are unexpectedly taken away.

Suddenly, Evelyn's wise words sprung into my mind. "You see, there is always a lesson to be learned, or an opportunity to show kindness, my dear. No matter the circumstance. And often times, a situation is neither good nor bad, but our thinking and how we respond to it makes it so."

In that moment, I found myself thankful for this experience. I knew, without a shadow of a doubt, that I had learned a lesson. With a simple shift of perception, all had changed. This unforeseen adventure had already taught me so much, and I knew that it had forever impacted my outlook on life, for the better.

We pulled up by the curb at the airport drop-off and all seemed like a déjà vu. People rushing, doors slamming, cars honking, all was the same except for the fact that there was absolutely no airborne activity. As far as I could tell, no one else had noticed.

We stepped through the airport doors, and it was as if we had just entered a giant, heated beehive. People were lined up by the masses at every open counter while others paced around eager for any kind of news. Janie paused and brought us close to her side.

"There's a lot of people in here. Let's make sure we stay together, understood?" All three of us nodded. "Okay, let's go."

Out of the kindness of his heart, David made himself temporary owner of one of my aunt's oversized suitcases. I sighed in relief, having to haul only two of my own.

With swift steps, Janie confidently made her way through the crowd, clearing a small path for us to follow. After weaving along with her endlessly saying, "Excuse me," and "Pardon me," we were now standing at the end of Canadian Air's service line.

"How long do you think we'll have to wait?" David asked, fanning himself with his shirt.

"As long as it takes for someone to tell us we're going home," Janie answered confidently.

I couldn't help but wonder. *Were we really going home today? If there's no airborne activity, how in the world are we going to get there? I guess we won't. At least not until tomorrow . . . this is so annoying. And why does it have to be so hot in here? Ugh! We're going to need to haul all our suitcases back into a cab again and*—STOP!

That word had pierced through my thoughts so loud that it had startled me. A name flashed across my mind: *Clarisse.* Reliving this morning's scene, I recalled all her bitter complaints. It dawned on me that I was recognizing parts of her in myself. I winced.

Stop! The inner voice stated again, and this time, Evelyn's calm, positive, and poised figure took center stage. Almost instantaneously, my wince transformed into a warm, genuine smile and it was at that moment that I realized which of the two sisters I wanted to be.

I couldn't believe how easy it had been for me to fall into a negative cycle. How naïve it was to internally gripe and complain. I had made myself both sad and happy as a result of two different thoughts. *Why?*

I didn't know the answer, but one thing had made itself clear; from now on, I would consciously choose to see the good in every situation. I would elect to be positive no matter the condition. I was, without a shadow of a doubt, deciding to become more like the Evelyns of the world.

CHAPTER 9

A SPARK OF HOPE

"Hi, my name is Silvia. May I have your final destination and full name, please?"

The representative smiled, and Janie gladly gave her the information requested. After a few *clicks* of the mouse, Silvia looked up from her computer screen.

"Checking any bags?"

"Yes, these three," Janie said, signaling for David and Lindsey to bring their bags forward. At the press of a button, she pulled out three printed luggage tags and slapped them onto each suitcase.

"Alright, your flight's departure is scheduled for 5 p.m. from Gate A13. You'll be seated together in Row 33. Other than that, you guys are all set."

"Oh, thank goodness! Thank you so much," Janie stated relieved.

"My pleasure. Is there anything else I can help you with?"

"Yes, actually, would it be possible to make sure that this little girl is seated next to us?" Janie asked, wrapping her arm around my shoulder. "She was traveling by herself, and well, until I can get her safely to her family, she's one of mine."

"Of course." Silvia nodded. "That's very sweet of you. And you, little girl, are very lucky. Let me see what I can do. May I have your full name please, sweetie?" As soon as I answered, Janie spoke again.

"If you have to separate us, two and two, that would be fine as well . . . "

Silvia grinned but kept her eyes on her screen. A few more *clicks* went by before she spoke again.

"Okay Mrs. Mitchell, I think you will be pleased. Lucy is seated in 33D. Same row as you guys, just on the other side of the aisle. Does that work?"

"Thank you so much!" I answered, relieved.

"Oh, yes, that works great! Thank you so much for your help and thank you for being so kind. I know your job can't be easy with all this chaos, but we truly do appreciate your kindness," Janie stated.

"Oh, no problem at all. Besides, what's the worth in only showing kindness when it's easy, right?" She winked before turning her attention to me. "And how many bags are you checking in today, hon?"

"These last three," I mumbled.

As Silvia worked her magic on the computer, it suddenly dawned on me, *Oh my goodness, yes! Hallelujah! Her computer is actually working!* The more I thought about it, the more excited I became. By the time she finally handed me my ticket, it took all I had in me not to do a victory dance. As my fingers ran over the black ink, I gasped in excitement knowing that what we had all been longing for was finally becoming a reality. I had only one thing left on my mind: getting home.

After clearing security and settling near our gate, Lindsey and I headed on a quest to find the nearest payphone.

"So, do you think everything's back to normal now with the computers working and all?" I asked.

"No, I don't think so. I overheard someone saying that only part of the city's electricity has been reinstated . . . He said that other parts would likely be out for weeks."

"For weeks?!" I exclaimed. "Whoa. I don't know how they managed to make this part of town work, but I sure am glad things are looking up for us."

"You and me both. And speaking of looking up, I spy with my little eye . . . "

Buying into her game, I quickly spotted the payphone. At the sight of the long line, I sighed. Remembering the commitment I had made to see the good in every situation, I finished Lindsey's sentence, "Something that will help us pass time." I smiled, nudging her in the arm.

"Yeah, I guess," she answered. "Besides, all that's truly left to do before boarding the plane is wait anyway, so why not."

"Yep. About five hours left to go," I stated, taking my place in line.

After a grueling thirty minutes, it was my turn to pick up the receiver. Confidently, I dialed my calling card and the correct phone number. *Ring, ring, click.*

"Hello?"

"Hi, Sue. It's Lucy. Is my Mom or Dad near you?"

"Oh, hi dear! How are you? Your mom was driving me absolutely nuts, so I sent her and your dad to the mall about an hour ago. She needed the distraction, and I needed some sanity. I told her I would stay behind just in case you called. Anyway, do you know when you'll get here?"

"Wow, I am shocked! How did you manage that?"

"Ha! Well, long story short, I gave her a choice, retail therapy or a Xanax. She caught my drift, gathered herself and headed out the door. As simple as that."

I laughed.

"Anyway, what's the scoop, kiddo?"

"Well, I have good news. Part of the city's electricity has returned and both me and the people I've been staying with were all able to get our boarding passes."

"Oh, that's great news! So, when are you guys supposed to take off?"

"Well, I haven't seen any airborne activity yet, but they told us 5 p.m."

"Okay so, 5 p.m. takeoff, plus the flight time, plus the time difference, you are looking at . . . " The line went silent as Sue did the math. "Around 9:30 p.m. then?"

"Yeah, somewhere around there, I think."

"Okay, great! I will let your parents know. I'll also make sure to double check with the local airport for any updates or changes."

"That's a great idea. Thank you so much."

"Listen, don't worry about us. I've got your mom pretty much under control, so you just concentrate on getting yourself back here safe and sound, young lady."

"Sounds good." I giggled. "I'll see you guys around 9:30 p.m."

"See you then, sweetheart. Have a safe flight." *Click.*

As I hung the phone back onto the receiver, I smiled happily.

"I'm glad that went well," Lindsey said brightly.

"You and me both," I answered, pivoting on my heels.

By the time we rejoined Janie and David, nearly an hour had passed.

"There you are! It's about time," David said, tapping his watch. "What took you guys so long anyway? I was starting to get worried."

"Ehh, have you not noticed the number of people in this place?" Lindsey answered. "So you can imagine the number of people waiting in line for that payphone."

"Yeah, I guess . . . " he shrugged.

Janie chuckled and shook her head. "Lucy, were you able to get in touch with your parents?"

"Ehh, not quite. My parents were out of the house, but I did speak with their friend, Sue, and she said she would fill them in."

"Okay, good. Our bases are now covered, and all we have left to do is wait." She smiled.

As we waited, I got to learn more about this amazing family. We covered get-to-know-you subjects from favorite movies to biggest fears. I learned that David was studying to become a teacher and that Lindsey aimed to become a psychologist. As for me, I was just about to begin high school and the idea of selecting a permanent profession had barely crossed my mind. However, the thought of being in college seemed so distant and yet so close. The possibilities were endless.

All of us jumped in surprise when someone shouted into a handheld intercom, and the whole terminal became silent.

"Thank you so much for your attention. As you all know, some of the power has been restored locally and luckily for us, parts of our systems are functioning, which is why we were able to issue you your boarding passes. Unfortunately, the air signal to our towers which directs and permits takeoff and landing is still temporarily out of service." Disappointment hung in the air as the agent took a breath. "However, we have a crew diligently working to resolve that issue, and as soon as we get the green light, we will do our best to get you guys boarded and on your way."

"So chances are we're not taking off today then?" someone stated from the back.

"Look, I would be lying if I told all of you that going home today is a guarantee, but I assure you that this is our utmost priority. We are using all available resources to reinstate aerial communication and as soon as we succeed, we will get you home. With this being said, I would like to personally thank all of you for being so patient and understanding. Folks, we will figure this out. It's only a matter of time. Thank you."

The agent smiled and the atmosphere within the terminal changed. As he stepped down from his footstool, someone shouted, "Thank you!" Someone else shouted, "We appreciate you guys!"

People started clapping, whistling, and cheering, creating a snowball effect and before we knew it, the sound of genuine encouragement and support was echoing from the walls and roaring within our ears. What a sight and what a feeling. In that very moment, I understood the true meaning of community.

"Are we still leaving at 5?"

"Did they reestablish communication with the towers?"

"Will we still get home today?"

"When are they going to update us?"

People around us were asking questions, and I wondered the same. It had been an hour and a half since our last update and strangely no one had returned to check on us since. This wasn't a good sign.

By the time 4:45 rolled around, everyone at Gate A13 had concluded that we would, in fact, not be going home today. Choosing to think differently, I knew that this was the home stretch.

I looked out of the airport window onto the runway, and to my surprise and delight, an airplane had just landed. Excitement sparked within my stomach, and I was at a loss for words. Almost simultaneously, a semi-familiar voice took over the loud speaker.

"May I have your attention, please?" The constant buzz that lingered among us vanished instantaneously. "I have some good news and some bad news . . . For starters, as most of you have figured out by now, it is with great regret that I have to inform you that your plane will not be taking off by 5:00 today." The crowd groaned. "However, the good news is that we've re-established aerial communication with our main tower, which is why some of you may have noticed some runway activity. Now that our means of communication have been restored," he paused with a grin, "we will begin the boarding process in no more than forty-five minutes."

For the second time that day, the crowd erupted into a cheer.

People immediately stood to line up in front of our gate. The fact that the agents weren't quite ready to serve us didn't matter.

"Ladies and gentlemen, may I have your attention please?" A female voice shouted from the front of the line.

I looked up at the Canadian Air agent who was standing tall atop the counter.

"Thank you. Okay, since we want to get you guys home as soon as possible, we ask that you please have your boarding pass ready and your passport open to your picture page. Also, as an extra precautionary step, we will manually cross-reference your legal documents with our master sheet. We understand that this may take a few more minutes than the typical boarding process, but at this point we, want to eliminate any other potential delay. I want to sincerely thank all of you for your attention, and we would like to begin boarding with passengers seated in rows 1 through 10. Thank you."

As people shuffled in and out of the line repositioning themselves, Janie, David, Lindsey and I fell to the back of the queue.

"How long do you think this will take?" David asked resting his arm on his mom's shoulder.

"My guess, anywhere from forty-five minutes to an hour," she stated.

David sighed. He was getting antsy, and so were the rest of us.

Through all of this, I wondered how it had been possible for all Canadian Air agents to remain so calm, genuine, and nice. Granted, a part of me suspected that they had received specific instructions from their management, but nonetheless, they had embraced an honest sense of service. The fact was that they were excelling at their job in a difficult environment surrounded by uncontrollable circumstances. Where some had seen misfortune and bad luck, they had seen potential and opportunity.

It became clear to me that by some sort of internal pull, they had made a choice. They had consciously chosen patience over intolerance, service over laziness, and sincerity over indifference.

CHAPTER 10

A NEW PERSPECTIVE

It was hard for me to describe the feeling of my behind making firm contact with my seat's faux leather. Relief, excitement, eagerness, and enthusiasm had all merged into one.

The pilot's voice welcomed us over the intercom and the stirring reality of what was about to happen became even more concrete.

This is it! I thought, butterflies surging at the pit of my stomach, *we are finally going home*!

I looked across the aisle at Lindsey, who was grinning from ear to ear, and I shared her excitement.

Our plane pulled away from the airport, and we taxied for what seemed like an eternity. Just as I thought we were finally getting ready to soar, my heart dropped at the oh-so- familiar sound of the *ding*.

"Ladies and gentlemen, I would just like to inform you that—" *No. Oh please no*, I thought, the palm of my hands sweating, *let us go home today*. "—we are third in line for takeoff so five to ten more minutes and we should be airborne. Thank you for your patience." I let out a deep sigh of relief. *Thank you,* I whispered under my breath, *thank you.*

At the ten-minute mark, the plane's engine revved from underneath us, and we began picking up speed. *Bring it on,* I thought, gripping my armrests.

Gradually the airplane tilted upwards, compressing us down into our seats and finally, we were airborne. So much happiness and excitement coursed through my veins. The thrill of flying and my eagerness to get home had me grinning from ear to ear.

By the time we reached cruising altitude, the sun had already begun setting. Between the prolonged boarding process and the delay in takeoff, I had lost all track of time. I looked at my watch; it was nearing 8:30 p.m.

I immediately thought about Sue and my parents. *I hope they checked with the local airport before driving over there.* I was bummed that I couldn't give them a second update. The more I put myself in their shoes, the worse I felt. This had been nothing more than an excruciating waiting game for them and they were no doubt running out of patience.

Stop that, Lucy. Don't worry. The minute you land, all their worries will go away. What will matter most to them is that you got home safe and sound, the voice in my head stated. I smiled and the feeling of guilt that had slyly tried to settle within me, vanished.

From three seats over, I watched the sunset. The bright, bold colors were a delight. I had never seen anything like it, and from this high up, it was a complete treat. The more I watched, the more thankful I felt.

I began thinking about everything that had happened, from being dropped off by my uncle on that early Thursday morning, up till now. It blew my mind to discover just how much I had learned about life, other people, and most importantly, myself. I had started this return trip as a young innocent girl flying for the second time and now, here I was inwardly transformed. In the last 36 hours, I had developed a new pair of eyes, gained a new perception of the world, and had grown, not in years, but in maturity. *You are a very lucky girl, Lucy*, the voice in my head stated.

The colors that painted the sky began fading, making way for the night, and suddenly my eyelids grew heavy. I shook my head in a feeble attempt to fight it, but it was too late. I closed my eyes and began drifting. *What a trip. What a lesson. What an adventure . . .*

My drowsy body was jerked forward, and I immediately jolted awake.

Ding.

"Ladies and gentlemen, welcome to Moncton."

Still half asleep and slightly confused, I rubbed my eyes. *Did he just say what I think he said?* I thought, slowly processing.

The passengers instantly began cheering, clapping, hooting, and hollering. *Oh my goodness, we are here!* I thought, suddenly wide-awake.

I looked across the aisle at the Mitchell family who were brimming with excitement. What we had all been waiting for was here at last. We were finally home.

It didn't take long after the seatbelt sign was removed for passengers to flood the aisle. Row by row, the seats in front of us emptied until it was our turn.

"Guys, we are here. We are ACTUALLY here!" Lindsey stated, her voice cracking with enthusiasm.

She wasted no time stepping into the aisle and making her way towards the front of the plane. Before following behind her, David stepped out of his row and gave me a firm high-five.

"We made it!" he stated. I couldn't help but laugh.

"Go ahead." Janie nodded for me to step in front of her. "I'm sure your parents are beyond eager to see you," she added, patting me on the shoulder.

At that moment, I imagined the expression of anticipation on my parents' faces, and I knew they would be eagerly expecting me. Urgently and with excitement, I began making my way up the aisle. I wondered how many other families had suffered what my parents had gone through.

At the front of the plane, our flight attendant's bright, chipper voice brought me out of my thoughts.

"Thank you for flying Canadian Air. Have a great night."

Despite it being nearly midnight, her smile was genuine, and I couldn't stop myself from reciprocating.

Here we go, I thought, stepping out onto the staircase and into the night. The air was cool and refreshing. *Home, sweet home.* My heart pounded out of excitement and a part of me wanted to sprint forward to meet my parents.

As I entered the airport, people waiting in the terminal buzzed with anticipation. I imagined my parents impatiently scanning each arriving passenger.

"Are you excited?" Lindsey asked.

"Me? Nah, not at all," I laughed, trying to play it cool.

"I sure am!" Janie said, passing us by.

Without a second thought, we wasted no time catching up with her.

As we turned the corner and entered the baggage claim area, we came face to face with a crowd of people waiting to be reunited with their loved ones. Overwhelmed, I quickly began scanning the room in search of a familiar face.

"Is that them?" Lindsey asked, elbowing me in the ribs. At the sight of waving arms, I blushed.

"Yeah, that's them," I answered with a smile.

Thinking that we hadn't yet spotted them, my mother decided to take matters into her own hands.

"Lucy, over here!" she shouted.

Her voice had managed to pierce through the entire chatter. Slightly embarrassed, I gave her a quick wave and speedily covered the ground between us in order to avoid a second holler.

The very second I came within reach of my mother's arms, she yanked me in for a firm, long-awaited hug.

"Oh thank God you're home safe!" she exclaimed. "Thank God!"

After a few seconds, I attempted to pull myself away from her grip, but to no avail.

"Caryn, she made it all the way here safe and sound, so please don't kill her now," Sue said from over my shoulder. Against her will, my mother reluctantly released her hold on me. "Finally, your dad and I can get a turn," she added with a smirk. I laughed.

Their life-long friendship had really been put to the test these last few days.

With pursed lips, my mom took a step back and my dad greeted me with a hug and a kiss.

"As you can tell, your mom was really worried about you. In fact, we all were."

Before I could even reply, Sue slid in for a quick hug and nodded for me to introduce the Mitchells who were patiently standing behind me. Slightly ashamed that I had, for a moment, neglected them, I cleared my throat.

"Mom, Dad, Sue, meet Janie, David, and Lindsey, the wonderful family that took me under their wings."

Smiling, Janie extended her hand to my mom, but to her surprise, was pulled in for an immediate hug.

While my mom was squeezing her tight, my dad took David's hand and Sue hugged Lindsey.

I took a step back and watched as parts of my world collided. My heart began bursting with joy. At that moment, I found myself in awe at the beauty of seeing pure strangers bonding.

As that tender scene unfolded, it occurred to me that I had, in sort, done the same thing. I thought about when I first saw the Mitchells, to that moment when I deemed them good people, to that instant when I chose to smile back at them.

At the time, I had no way of knowing that a simple, sincere gesture would bring me such comfort and relief, or that a sprinkle of faith would bring forth trust and friendship. There was no way to foresee that an act of genuine kindness would bloom into an everlasting bond.

As I stood there, a familiar voice pierced my thoughts *'You see my dear, you truly do reap what you sow.'*

My mind connected the dots; and for the first time, I understood the real meaning behind Evelyn's wise words. Overwhelmed by this sudden revelation, I knew that she had given me insight into something far greater than I ever knew existed, something that reached far beyond my years, something precious that I would cherish forever: she had given me a new perspective on life.

Years have passed since that event, and since then, I've often heard that there is no substitute for experience. Looking back, I can agree. The wisdom I gained and the lessons I learned from that trip are some of my most treasured assets. From showing kindness to braving the unknown, I was exposed to some of life's precious lessons.

To this day, the Mitchells and I are still in contact. The everlasting impact they had on my life is one that I will never forget, and one that I hold dear to my heart.

To you three, my guardian angels, thank you for taking me under your wings. Thank you for trusting your instincts, and thank you for making me one of your own.

To my younger self, I am proud of the choices you've made and of the lessons you were open to learning.

And to you, the adventurer, I hope that this story has inspired you to be brave, to have faith, to trust, and to be kind.

Remember: life is the teacher and we need only to listen with our hearts to discover the things she wishes for us to uncover.

To your next adventure,

Lucy

Made in the USA
San Bernardino, CA
11 November 2019

59725374R10066